D0563798

Monticello in Mind

Monticello in Mind

Fifty Contemporary Poems on Jefferson

Edited by Lisa Russ Spaar

UNIVERSITY OF VIRGINIA PRESS

Charlottesville & London

University of Virginia Press
© 2016 by the Rector and Visitors of the University of Virginia
All rights reserved
Printed in the United States of America on acid-free paper

First published 2016
ISBN 978-0-8139-3850-9

9 8 7 6 5 4 3 2 1

Library of Congress Cataloging-in-Publication Data
is available from the Library of Congress.

For
Carol Muske-Dukes
and
In Memoriam
Claudia Emerson

Among my many colleagues in the University of Virginia's Department of English whose fruitful conversations about and support of this project have been invaluable, I thank, particularly, Steve Arata, Anna Brickhouse, Stephen Cushman, John O'Brien, Brad Pasanek, Cynthia Wall, and June Webb. I'm grateful to the University of Virginia Press for finding this anthology a publishable endeavor, and want to thank especially my editor, Boyd Zenner, and the Press director, Mark Saunders. Morgan Myers provided discerning, scrupulous copy-editing of the manuscript. My appreciation goes, as well, to the staff of the Albert and Shirley Small Special Collections Library, notably Anne Causey and George Riser. Several anonymous readers of this book's proposal at the early stages made invaluable suggestions for which I am also grateful. Jonathan Grossman offered helpful insights into Jefferson's poetry scrapbooks, and Director Leslie Bowman and Curator Susan Stein at the Monticello Foundation have been supportive since the project's inception. The knowledgeable, generous Emilie Johnston was a delightful cicerone on an unforgettable evening tour of Monticello one stormy August evening during the making of this book. This project would not have been possible without generous support from an Arts, Humanities, and Social Sciences Research Grant from the College of Arts and Sciences at the University of Virginia; from the Jefferson Scholars Foundation, which honored me with its Faculty Award for 2013–15; and from a fellowship at the Virginia Foundation for the Humanities. Finally, I offer my great gratitude to the poets included in this book, many of whom undertook the daunting and difficult task of writing poems expressly for this anthology. To paraphrase Thomas Jefferson, I cannot live without your words.

As the classically trained Thomas Jefferson would have known, the word *poet* derives from the Greek *poetes* ("maker"), from *poein* ("to make, create, compose"). Jefferson was himself a consummate and complicated maker—a compulsive builder and tearer-down and refashioner of houses; a fluent forger of declarations, laws, statutes, nations; the founder of two institutions of higher education, West Point and the University of Virginia; an amateur and innovator in realms as various as gardening and vaccination, viticulture and surveying, beekeeping and Biblical scholarship, architecture and muslins. The author of one incomplete autobiography, Jefferson was also a conjurer of selves—a creator of truths and a creator of fictions. Perhaps because of a habit formed after a fire burned to the ground his childhood home, he became an obsessive copier, list maker, collector, and record keeper—an eloquent, prolific writer of public addresses, papers, ledgers, accountings, and thousands of letters.

Although Jefferson wrote, in an 1813 letter to the grammarian John Waldo, that "mine has been a life of business," he was for most of his life a catholic and ardent reader of poetry. His tastes ranged from what he called the "ductile and copious language" of Homer and Virgil (whom he regarded as "the rapture of every age and nation") to the sentimental and patriotic verses published in the newspapers and poetry anthologies of his day. He was the subject of many poems in his lifetime, some praising him but others taking bold potshots at his politics and his personal life, including his relationship with his slave Sally Hemings. While a student of the law at William and Mary, he kept a commonplace book in which he copied out aphorisms, epigrams, and passages of verse (much of it betraying his difficulties with women). Years later, he composed an essay titled "Thoughts on English Prosody" (1786), in which, among other assertions, he declared that "the accent shall never be displaced from the syllable . . . [in] English verse," that "no two persons will accent the same passage alike," and that in blank verse the poet, "unfettered by rhyme, is at liberty to prune his diction of those tautologies, those feeble nothings necessary to introtude [*sic*] the rhyming word."

Poetry and literature also formed an important medium for Jefferson's closest relationships. He often clipped and sent poems written by others to his family members and friends. For instance, in 1808 he sent his granddaughter Cornelia a stanza he encountered as an adolescent from *Thomas White's Little Book for Little Children*. It's not hard to imagine Jefferson seeing himself in both the witness and the vision depicted in this bit of verse:

> I've seen the sea all in a blaze of fire
> I've seen a house high as the moon and higher
> I've seen the sun at twelve o'clock at night
> I've seen the man who saw this wondrous sight.

Years earlier, when Jefferson's wife Martha was dying in September of 1782, she and Jefferson copied out, as verse, these lines from Laurence Sterne's novel *The Life and Opinions of Tristam Shandy*: first, in Martha's hand, "Time wastes too fast; every letter / I trace tells me with what rapidity life follows my pen. The days and hours / of it are flying over our heads like clouds of a windy day never to return"; and then in Jefferson's, "and every time I kiss thy hand to bid adieu, every absence which / follows it, are preludes to the eternal separation which we are shortly to make!" Jefferson was to keep this paper, wrapped with a lock of Martha's hair, for the remainder of his life.

Only one surviving poem can be attributed with certainty to the pen of Jefferson himself, an "adieu" to his daughter Martha, composed just before his death:

> Life's visions are vanished, it's dreams are no more.
> Dear friends of my bosom, why bathed in tears?
> I go to my fathers; I welcome the shore,
> which crowns all my hopes, or which buries my cares.
> Then farewell my dear, my lov'd daughter, Adieu!

The last pang in life is in parting from you.
Two Seraphs await me, long shrouded in death;
I will bear them your love on my last parting breath.

But as Kevin J. Hayes points out in *The Road to Monticello: The Life and Mind of Thomas Jefferson* (2008), transcriptions from Jefferson's Garden Book ledger themselves "read almost like modern verse," as in this page of entries from the spring of 1766:

Purple hyacinth begins to bloom.
Narcissus and Puckoon open.
Puckoon flowers fallen.
a bluish colored, funnel-formed flower in lowgrounds in bloom
purple flag blooms. Hyacinth and Narcissus are gone.
Wild honeysuckle in our woods open.—also the Dwarf flag & Violets
blue flower in low grounds vanished.
The purple flag, Dwarf flag, Violet & wild Honeysuckle still in bloom.

In the last decade of his life, Jefferson conceived of and laid the cornerstone for the University of Virginia, where students were able to study a traditional curriculum of law, medicine, and divinity, but also a panoply of other disciplines that included modern and ancient languages, rhetoric, belles lettres, and the fine arts. Rather than surrounding a church or chapel, which was typical at the time, the Grounds of the University were to have as their locus the Rotunda, designed by Jefferson on the model of the Pantheon in Rome and meant to house a library, a "circular room for . . . books" in Jefferson's words, that would be largely supplied, initially, from his personal collection. The Rotunda was not completed until after Jefferson's death, but it is clear that Jefferson meant to place books and writing, including poetry, rather than religion, at the center of his "academical village." According to Andrew K. Smith, in an account of Jefferson's funeral written some fifty years after the event (15 October 1875), among those early University of Virginia students gathered at the Monticello grave site to pay respects to the University's deceased founder was the poet Edgar Allan Poe, "a high-minded and honorable young man, though easily persuaded to his wrong."

Jefferson, during his presidency, subscribed to at least two anthologies of verse and also assembled and occasionally lightly annotated a remarkable scrapbook of poems that he encountered, primarily as a prodigious reader of newspapers. Jonathan Gross, in his introduction to *Thomas Jefferson's Scrapbooks: Poems of Nation, Family, and Romantic Love Collected by America's Third President* (2006), says that poetry, his own and others', was a critical way in which Jefferson "communicat[ed] with those he loved." In particular, the poems Jefferson collected for his own and his granddaughters' scrapbooks while president, Grossman says, "form a portrait of his age and offer, by contrast, a portrait of our own. If a verse seems sentimental and cloying, trivial or charming, it illustrates how our attitudes toward nation, family, and poetry itself have changed: the poems read us."

Monticello in Mind, an anthology of poems by fifty contemporary poets representing a wide range of cultural and aesthetic perspectives and all engaging in some way with Thomas Jefferson, is offered in this spirit. How do twentieth- and twenty-first-century poets "read" Thomas Jefferson—in his time and in ours? How does Jefferson appear to interpret *us* in these poems even as we attempt to translate, illuminate, talk back to, and puzzle over *him*—his legacy, his genius, his achievements, his polarizing complexities, his hypocrisies and paradoxes, his hubris and failures, his vision of the American experiment? How, by extension, might poetry's innate stereoscopy reveal anew—with Jefferson as lens or point of resistance—our nation in the late middle age of its democracy, in our moment? What might such a project reveal about *us,* personally and as a culture? About poetry itself?

Jefferson was, after all, perhaps foremost among his many gifts, a writer. He had a knack and a love for what Michael Knox Beran, in *Jefferson's Demons: Portrait of a Restless Mind* (2007), calls the "broidery of words." He was so valued for his skill as a writer that his fellow Founding Fathers chose him to draft the document evincing the new nation's hopes and "self-evident" truths. Jefferson's real poetry, in fact, may reside in his memorable drafts of legislation and his speeches—even the Declaration of Independence was written to be read aloud—and it is on the strength of those writings that Beran calls Jefferson our "second-best political poet," naming Lincoln as the first. Jefferson's last physical gestures, on his deathbed, were of writing in the air. Of course what Jefferson *did* put into writing during his lifetime is as troublesome to some as it is prophetic, and what he chose *not* to record, in the course of his public and personal life, is as powerful as what he articulated. The poets in this book move into those declarations and into that silence, offering new and immediate voice to both.

Conception

This anthology had its incipient glimmer a decade and a half ago. The poet Carol Muske-Dukes was in residence at the University of Virginia for a week in the spring of 1999 as the Rea Visiting Writer, and as has been the case with many of our visiting poets over the years—Seamus Heaney, Mark Strand, and Allen Ginsberg, to name but a few—Carol was interested in visiting Monticello. In my then capacity as director of the University of Virginia Creative Writing Program, it was my privilege and pleasure to ferry her there and to enjoy a special, private house tour arranged by my friend, Monticello senior curator Susan Stein.

Our docent that rainy afternoon let us roam a bit on our own, so we made our way up one of the narrow staircases to the beautiful, sky-lit dome room. As we stood in that place and gazed out of its round windows at the pastel beds of tulips, the emerald lap of lawn, at Mulberry Row where the plantation's enslaved people lived, and further out over the Blue Ridge Mountains, we talked about Jefferson's paradoxes, his insatiable curiosity, his blind spots, his prescience, his secrets.

Carol said that the house felt like an embodiment of the man himself, with its private and its public spaces, its ambages, its honeycomb of underground work areas. (In *Jefferson and Monticello: The Biography of a Builder,* Jack McLaughlin writes: "Those who construct their own shelter replicate themselves, at their deepest and most significant level, in their houses. They *are* what they build.") We agreed that the house, "haunted" as it was by Jefferson and his family, slaves, and friends, was also in many ways like a poem—layered, figurative, difficult, suggestive, complex. We recalled poems we knew about Jefferson—Robert Penn Warren's *Brother to Dragons*, Philip Levine's "A Walk with Tom Jefferson," May Sarton's "Monticello," and poems about Monticello by Lucille Clifton, Robert Hass, and Yusef Komunyakaa. Karl Shapiro's "University" ("To hurt the Negro and avoid the Jew / Is the curriculum . . .") also came to mind, as did Ezra Pound's *Jefferson and/or Mussolini* and his fragments of Jefferson's writing in the *Cantos*.

I am indebted to Carol for helping to conceive this book that April afternoon, which, we later learned, by coincidence, was Founder's Day, the 256th anniversary of Jefferson's birth. Her poem included in this anthology offers an account of that visit we made together. This book is dedicated to her, and to the memory of Claudia Emerson, who tragically died while it was being assembled.

A couple of years ago, when I finally got around to conceptualizing this anthology in earnest, I decided that rather than take a chronological, historic, or comprehensive approach to the subject, I would "commission" new poems from fifty contemporary poets, inviting them to respond in any way that interested them to Thomas Jefferson. With a few exceptions, then, the poems included in this book have been written expressly for the project. The choice to solicit only fifty poems, mainly unpublished, means that several rich, provocative poems about Jefferson and Monticello are left out, among them some of the aforementioned poems (including satirical verses about Jefferson published during his lifetime) as well as recent work by Mary Jo Bang, Eve Shockley, and others. I placed no restrictions on the participating poets in terms of aspect, style, scope, or length, trusting that the fifty writers—each with his or her various aesthetic, stylistic, and topical inclinations—would, individually and in total, not only create a fascinating portrait of Jefferson in our moment but would also bring into juxtaposition a range of twentieth- and twenty-first-century poetic responses to an iconic figure that might reverberate provocatively with the American experience. I was right to trust that instinct.

The Poems

> Historical sense and poetic sense should not, in the end, be contradictory, for if poetry is the little myth we make, history is the big myth we live, and in our living, constantly remake.
>
> —Robert Penn Warren, from the 1953 foreword to *Brother to Dragons*

> A poem I write is not just about me; it is about national identity, not just regional but national, the history of people in relation to other people. I reach for these outward stories to make sense of my own life, and how my story intersects with a larger public history.
>
> —Natasha Trethewey, from a 2008 interview

If, as Jonathan Grossman said of Jefferson's poetry scrapbooks, "the poems read us," what do these fifty poems by fifty contemporary poets reveal—about Jefferson's legacy, about America and Americans, about the myth we make of history and of ourselves? I want the poems to express their own truths, but annotations of each poem accompany the poets' biographies at the back of this volume. What I want to offer here is an overview of the whole collection, and the reader will discern that nearly all of life is represented here. The lenses of these poems—some personal, some cultural, some historical, many all three—concern, variously, family (acknowledged and unacknowledged), nation, empire, race, time, class, religion, gender, politics, love, the environment, and even poetry itself; and are by turns ironic, angry, admiring, bemused, distanced, intimate, frustrated, hopeful. Representing diverse generic and aesthetic modes (dramatic, lyric, narrative; experimental and traditional) as well as a range of cultural perspectives, the poems show us how so many of the same issues that vexed the newly forged nation abide and are, in inextricable ways, connected with one another.

As might be expected, a good number if not all of these poems address, directly or obliquely, issues of power, particularly in relation to race, that are ongoing in American culture. The speaker of Ravi Shankar's "Thomas Jefferson in Kathmandu," for instance, addresses Jefferson from across distances of time and place:

> I'm on the other side of the world and still
>   can't see clearly what has succeeded and what failed
>   in the grand American experiment. I eat my fill,
>
> no prayer bowl to beg from, yet have been jailed
>   and bailed out, slurred, even refused service at a diner
>   250 years after you were born.

Joan Naviyuk Kane ponders, in "Incognitum," the "skeletons assembl[ed]" in Jefferson's Indian Hall ("evidence of someone / else's way through valleys dense, interior, and distant"), and worries about the voices of indigenous peoples lost forever to the movements of expansion and empire. Simon Ortiz speaks to this extinction in "Freedom and the Lie: Monticello and Thomas Jefferson: Plan," when he writes: "Freedom is never its own. Monticello constructed. / Simple as fact and act. Indigenous people and Mother Earth died." And though, as Natasha Trethewey writes in "Enlightenment," "much has changed," the personal history of her narrator's mixed-race heritage (and, by extension, the inheritance of African Americans in the United States) means that what "links us—white father, black daughter— / . . . renders us other to each other."

Gender is another concern of many of these poems, the complex mesh of authority and submission, for instance, that certainly shaped the lives of the women around Jefferson—not just his slaves, enslaved offspring, and enslaved mistress but also his white daughters, whom Jennifer Key calls, in "Jefferson's Daughters," "less blossom than bomb." Race and gender blend in Aracelis Girmay's "[*american verses,* excerpt]," in which the poet describes the experience of being a girl of color "exiled" in America:

> In 1771, part of me is here and part of me
> still coming: this, the body's best trick.

Already, one grandfather is laying the tracks
and one grandmother is picking coffee, and

one has not even heard, yet, this word "America."
To think I thought I knew nothing,

could say nothing about "America,"
so silently I was jennied into the country's spool.

Similarly, in "Daddy Hemmings was Good with Curves," Yusef
Komunyakaa shows how Jefferson's enslaved people, especially
those related to him, learned to "work / the saw with & against the
grain," compromising even private and domestic roles in order to
forge for themselves a legacy of freedom and agency. And in Car-
men Gillespie's "Monticello Duet: Outside/In," former Monticello
slave Isaac Jefferson and Sally Hemings speak in a part-transcribed,
part-imagined dialogue that reveals the irony of their situations as
enslaved people:

Isaac:
Isaac had to open the gates.
    Sally:
    ummm hmmm.

Illustrator and visual artist Maira Kalman has written, "If you
want to understand this country and its people and what it means
to be optimistic and complex and tragic and wrong and courageous,
you need to go to Monticello." Many of the poems here explore
the house that Jefferson (with the considerable contribution of his
family, employees, and slaves) spent most of his adult life imagining,
building, changing, demolishing, renovating, leaving, inhabiting,
and leaving, again, ultimately, to us, revealing it to be an emblem of
the profound paradoxes of the American experiment. Poems by Tal-
vikki Ansel, Gabrielle Calvocoressi, Jennifer Chang, Lucille Clifton,
Carol Muske-Dukes, Elizabeth Seydel Morgan, Nathaniel Perry,
Brian Teare, Willard Spiegelman, and others explore Jefferson's cre-
ated world on the "little mountain" (house, gardens, slave quarters,
woods, dome room), an "invention" that preoccupied Jefferson for

over thirty years. These pieces confirm, as novelist and radio host Kurt Anderson put it, that Monticello is "one of the places where America itself was dreamed up"—a site of passionate projection and idealization and a focal point for contradictory notions of American identity. Like Monticello, the nation (its populace, its identity, its poetry) was and is a collective work-in-progress. And part of that ongoing process involves a diving into the wreckage of our mangled imperial legacy, as Brenda Hillman does in "Near the Rim of the Ideal," a poem that riffs on the fact that "federal" is cognate with "faith" and explores what that might mean for America's "difficult daughters," alive in an exploitative culture: "my anarchist & I declare dependence / on the invisible, / & on its runt the visible . . . / not to hold these truths to be self-evident / if specifics fail."

I was not surprised, either, to find that a great number of these poems include Jefferson's own words and sample from his many texts (treatises, documents, letters), given that Jefferson was himself so eloquent but also that he was a figure whose identity was, in many respects, *made* of language—what he did and did not write, say, or record. Poems by Debra Allbery, Terrance Hayes, and Kiki Petrosino borrow intrepidly from Jefferson's own writing, often transforming his words into truths of which he himself may not have been aware. Particularly interesting are the number of poets (John Casteen, Stephen Cushman, Ron Slate, and David Wojahn) who chose to write about the Jefferson Bible, a project somewhat postmodern in its techniques of collage and erasure. The redacted Bible showed Jefferson's boldness (some might say hubris) in excising from the New Testament anything he thought to be beyond the realm of Enlightened fact, including Jesus's acts of miracle and any whiff of superstition or mystery. In a way, Jefferson's slicing and dicing of the Good Book foregrounds the processes by which much art is made, but as Stephen Cushman reminds us, "cutting and pasting / may deepen blindness, taste self-perpetuating handcuff itself, / got to paste in some challenges too."

Poems by Rita Dove, Thorpe Moeckel, Amy Newman, Ron Smith, and others revisit historical moments from Jefferson's life and, with the force of Paul Klee and Walter Benjamin's angel of history, breathe fresh life into the interstices of fact in order to reveal new truths about the full humanity of a complex man in his world and time. Other poems—those by Michael Collier, Claudia Emerson, Paisley Rekdal, Mary Ann Samyn, and R. T. Smith—use aspects of Jefferson's life (beekeeping, wine making, gardening, building, a habit of silence) to speak of the vexed legacy of his tireless and often oxymoronic enterprises. Paul Guest and Mark Jarman speak to two very different familial experiences of the Jefferson nickel. Nick Flynn, Lorine Niedecker, Debra Nystrom, Tracy K. Smith, and Larissa Szporluk use gender and the slippage of persona to speak to enduring issues of property, boundaries, inheritance, and power. Meanwhile, Maurice Manning wonders if Jefferson-the-rational ever had an epiphany, and Robert Hass imagines Jefferson scouring the aisles of the Charlottesville K-Mart for gadgets—"pulleys, levers, the separation of powers"—even as his narrator longs for a country in which powers are not separated, "one wing for Governor Randolph when he comes, / the other wing for love."

Still other poets meditate on Jefferson in order to articulate matters of personal, private significance. Tess Taylor, a white descendant of Jefferson, explores her family's legacy of culpability regarding slavery and other issues in "Graveyard, Monticello." In "Sight Lines," Arthur Sze, contemplating the geographical distance from Monticello to where he is walking in New Mexico, discovers that such imagining is a way to dispel the distance between himself and a loved one:

> I step out of the ditch but step deeper into myself—
> I arrive at a space that no longer needs autumn or spring—
> I find ginseng where there is no ginseng my talisman of desire—
> Though you are visiting Paris, you are here at my fingertips.

Gabriel Fried connects his own childhood experiences of New England orchards with those of Jefferson and his heirs, few of whom probably comprehended how bereft (financially and otherwise) Jefferson would leave them after his death. For Charles Wright in

"Christmas East of the Blue Ridge," Monticello stands in, metonymically, for a fin de siècle hunger for God and anxiety about the future. In "Reading a Biography of Thomas Jefferson in the Months of My Son's Recovery," Kate Daniels conflates Jefferson's paradoxes with the difficulties endured by her speaker and her speaker's bipolar son:

> Can't help drawing back at how he lived in two minds
> Because he was *of two minds* like a person
> With old time manic depression: the slaveholder
> And the Democrat, the tranquil hilltop of Monticello,
> And the ringing cobblestones of Paris, France. The white
> Wife, and the black slave mistress.

Among all of the provocative and beautiful poems compiled here, then, I hope that the reader discovers new ways of perceiving Jefferson, a person flawed and visionary and representing, as myth and man, many of the wordings and silences that continue both to plague and to sustain us as individuals, as Americans, and as poets. I would encourage readers to be alert to the ways in which these poems speak to one another, creating out of many voices one and out of one voice many—sometimes by the serendipity arising from my choice to arrange them alphabetically by the poets' surnames rather than thematically. This organization, I feel, allows for an illuminating pollination and what Cushman calls "spark" across poems. I love, for example, that the book begins with Debra Allbery's poem that locates Jefferson near the end of his life, in winter, scratching out a letter to an old friend, and ends with Kevin Young's poem about Phillis Wheatley, the first African American woman to publish a book of poetry, whom Jefferson was unable to see as worthy of the name of poet. Meanwhile, Young shows us Wheatley, like Allbery's Jefferson, in the act of writing. Speaking for Wheatley, Young writes, "My quill feather flies // Across the page. I wait." If Jefferson, in the words that Allbery borrows at the close of her poem, could, after death, return "once, after a while, to see how things have gone on," one hopes that he would be moved, stirred, and changed by the prismatic poems gathered here.

Monticello in Mind

An Ordinary Portion of Life

Jefferson to Adams, 1822

The life of the feeder, my dear Sir, is better
than that of the fighter. But I reach only my garden now,
and that with sensible fatigue. *With laboring step*
to tread our former footsteps, to beat and beat
the beaten track—it is surely not worth a wish.

I heard once a very old friend, who had troubled
himself with neither poets nor philosophers, say
much the same in plain prose—that he was tired
of pulling off his shoes and stockings every night
only to put them on again in the morning.

To pace the round eternal track, to taste
the tasted, decant another vintage—

to see what we have seen, dear friend. We have had,
you and I, more than an ordinary portion of life.

I shudder at the approach of winter, and wish
I could sleep through it with the dormouse.
The wish to stay here is thus gradually
extinguished—but not so easily that of returning,
once, after a while, to see how things have gone on.

from Works and Days

    (*Monticello*)

In September, the long stretch East: pockets
of mist in the hollows, fields; Shadwell, Kes-
wick, Tufton, twist of the Rivanna River.
Straightening up with candy wrappers,
a cigarette butt, some mornings I too
forgot where I was: Jefferson's
"sea view," white vapor rising; yellow sun
clearing the horizon, gilding everything,
for a moment, before the bustle of day.

    • • •

Twice now on the train I've passed below
the mountain where I used to work. The light
still soft at seven, before the tourists come; pink
hum of Apricot Beauty, blue *Mertensia,* Apeldoorn,
Queen of Sheba, Keizerskroon. Two robins
by the pond quarrel along an invisible line.
There's a puddle in the gravel walk by the stairs,
soon someone will bail it with
the dented coffee can, as they always have.

    • • •

"Stop," they say to each other "stop, I'll take
your photo." And stop, and stop. The two tulip
poplars frame the house: still green
with leaves, still standing, wired together,
a squirrel in one. A man holds a nickel up
to his face. Stop. What a shot, in front of the house.
Months later, the picture: squinting face,
tiny coin between finger and thumb; camcorder movies
of the gardener bent over, frowning in the sun.

    • • •

January. Arch of window against grey
sky, bright oranges on the citrus tree, helioptrope's
sweet smell from the slate floor. Behind me
in the house the guide says, "Mis*ter* Jefferson
woke every morning when the sun first hit
the clock above his bed." Boredom of cleaning seeds
in the workroom: flat Sweet William, prickly
poppy spines, shiny black columbine, in chaff—
cascade of love-lies-bleeding.

   ...

After the first spring, I think: never
to be surprised like this again. After months
of rain and snow, the mounded beds, and the fish
pond freezing—the quick
unfurling of color I cannot describe.
Blue of larkspur, a woman in a wheelchair
saying, "I feel the sun . . ." The old
roses: *Rosa chinensis,* 'Rosa mundi,' blooming
again, again unpruned.

Monticello Smokehouse Festivity

To be sung at high volume, by a large group, in rounds,
so the house shakes

Every house has a room the guests don't know. Yes.
Every house has a room the guests don't know. Belly
Deep beneath the shoes with their red leather soles.
Every house has a room the guests don't know.

Every house has a room where the hams get hung. Yes.
Every house has a room where the hams get hung. Belly
heavy from the places where the neighbor's hands go.
Every house has a room the guests don't know.

Every house has a room where the body can't fit. Yes.
Every house has a room where the body can't fit. Belly
Deep beneath the silences that fester and swell,
Every house has a room the guests don't know.

Every house has a room where the floor's still dirt. Yes.
Every house has a room where the floor's still dirt. Belly
Heaving on the ground and bruised where you fell.
Every house has a room that the guests don't know.

Every house has a room where the light can't get. Yes.
Every house has a room where the light can't get. Belly
Deep as a barrel beneath the shoulders' broken lintel.
Every house has a room that the guests don't know.

The Jefferson Bible

National Museum of American History, Washington, D.C.

I

"Politics as well as religion has its superstitions"

Having set aside his other tasks, he resolved
himself into the Word. Two volumes each
—face of any given page, and obverse—French,

English, Latin, Greek. Wheat paste, Japanese
shears, a hard needle pulling fine silk thread.
He fastened the chronology in place, cut

the filler, opened with taxation and the burden
of injustice. Imagine: that close work, knelt before
the altar of his writing desk—in view of the window,

gazing out across Mulberry Row, and townward.

II

Northeast Regional 176, near Rapidan, Virginia

One can anytime, in passing, write out poems
on a train. Beyond the window, the back side
of sidings, freight; ahead, the whistle dissembles.

Elsewhere, as we know, ordnance delivers itself
unto its destinations. No mercy. Two options
remain: to pursue one's own happiness without

harming others, or to hew to the hard and fast line
of a higher good. Two ideas. I can prefer neither.
At the crossroad, a plebiscite: the public wish: traffic.

The metaphor of travel connects us. And so on.

III

Thomas Jefferson Unitarian Universalist Church,
Rugby Road, Charlottesville

November: the bright lights of the sugar maples
blowing out. Each day feels like the end of history
but is not. Is *not*. You have to quit acting

like you don't know what you know. Above me,
the eye and vent of the oculus; a dome that directs
all sound down and into the ear, the innermost ear.

Others' voices reverberate in one's chest, here
in the temple of reason. His letters. His idea,
luminous and humanist. His handiwork, the Book

of the life. A compassion; a query. To hold open.

A Horse Named Never

At the stables, each stall was labeled with a name.

Biscuit stood aloof—I faced, always, invariably, his clockwork tail.

Crab knew the salt lick too well.

Trapezoid mastered stillness: a midnight mare, she was sternest and
    tallest, her chest stretched against the edges of her stall.

I was not afraid of Never, the chestnut gelding, so rode his iron
    haunches as far as Panther Gap.

Never and I lived in Virginia, then.

We could neither flee nor be kept.

Seldom did I reach the little mountain without him, its easy crests
    making valleys of indifferent grasses.

What was that low sound I heard, alone with Never?

A lone horse, a lodestar, a habit of fear.

*We think of a horse less as the history of one man and his sorrows than
    as the history of a whole evil time.*

Why I chose Never I'll never know.

He took me to the gardens overlooking this deplorable
    entanglement, our country.

I fed him odd lettuce, abundant bitterness.

Who wore the bit and harness, who was the ready steed.

Never took the carrot, words by my own reckoning, an account of
    creeks and oyster catchers.

Our hoof-house rested at the foot of the mountain, on which rested
    another house more brazen than statuary.

Let it be known: I first mistook gelding for gilding.

I am the fool that has faith in Never.

Somewhere, a gold door burdened with apology refuses all mint
from the yard.

monticello

(history: sally hemmings, slave at Monticello,
bore several children with bright red hair)

God declares no independence.
here come sons
from this black sally
branded with Jefferson hair.

Jefferson's Bees

They can cause you a lot of trouble and much pain,
these exotics known by natives as the white man's flies
but you wouldn't think of it as sorrow or grief,
all that joyful industry they seem to generate,
everyone doing a job, everyone, as my mother
used to say "at their rank and station." She who had
the orders of angels in mind, she who called
Brazil nuts, *nigger toes,* not all the time, though once
was enough to pass that thinking on to me.

    . . .

From his reading he noted Laplanders prepare pine bark
as a substitute for sugar and wondered how far north
bees might live, what routes of migration the harbingers
could survive ahead of the settlements.
No mention of the native *Bombus,* yellow banded,
scallop-winged and veined like beveled glass, not heliotropic
like the *Apis* but up and out at dawn, working
to the edge of night, grappling and hugging the stamens—
the flowers sometimes buckling from their weight.

    . . .

If then we can take from our Bees, a considerable
quantity of their superfluous Honey and Wax
without injuring them; if they will work for us
another, and many other Years, and every Year
pay us fair and reasonable Contributions; why
should we treat them with unnecessary Cruelty
and hurt Ourselves by a Greediness, that will turn
to our Prejudice? No true lover of Bees ever lighted
the fatal Match, that was to destroy his little Innocents.

If you guard them from Accidents, and save them from Poverty,
they will continue, by Succession, to the End of the World.

So it is written in "COLLATERAL BEE-BOXES: Or, a New,
Easy, and Advantageous Method of Managing Bees," 1757,
which Edmund Bacon, his overseer, who kept a stand
of more than forty hives, employed, although no records
detailing the perilous, sweet, invasive harvests survive,
only a sketch shows the boxes near the outhouses,
north and south, adjacent the poultry yards.

    • • •

Two centuries later, they stand east of the house, below
the Loop, four hives in an enclosure and two or three more
off to the side, less protected, a little beyond the greenhouses,
facing as they should sunrise, and, like everything
at Monticello, restored to an idea, one that's survived
its own foreclosure, having been based, at least
in the management of bees, on fostering spring swarms
while suppressing those in late summer, when the work
is complete and the workers vie for space with their honey.

Cut and Paste

If spirit whispers *Roll your own gospel,* who's to gainsay
cutting and pasting, Jefferson's life of Jesus for instance
delivers the kid, snips off his foreskin with eyelids shut tight
on star and magi, sore afraid shepherds, angels on high,
whatever's supernatural need not apply, no job for John
until the Last Supper, washing up feet, having served first
nothing comestible, nothing fermented, so much for supper,
much less remembrance, as for resurrection, what are you,
kidding, roll up the stone and that's all she wrote,
though Mr. Monticello keenly liked precepts, stories with morals
mostly from Matthew, lots of Luke too, and the comment on John
it turns out is wrong, he got the nod for cleansing the temple,
his woman caught cheating survived expurgation, big surprise
    there,
as did the teaching that being born blind's no proof of sin,
good thing for us, cutting and pasting's a natural process
of natural selection, who can do otherwise, we can't stick in all
the laughable fractions we even see, but cutting and pasting
may deepen blindness, taste self-perpetuating handcuff itself,
got to paste in some challenges too, censor the healings
you overlook the overlook and don't forget miracle
rhymes with empirical, he said it best, left to herself
truth'll do fine, nothing to fear from apparent confliction,
strike things together you might get a spark, maybe the one
you've long been awaiting, chant the Lord's Prayer
in Luke's version, fine, in Greek if you like, or Latin or French,
each column glued beside the King's English, but then follow up
with something unlikely, let's push the statute, let's worship freely,
Jaya Ganesha or the Tryambakam, mrityor mukshiya, free us from
    death
as a gourd from its stem, or worship like a Miwok climbing up
    through

the tonsure of tree line in springtime Yosemite, unknown by
    Jefferson,
hadn't been wrested from Mexico yet, then coming down
from altitude solitude, thin air's high chill, to granite dome faces
tear-stained with snowmelt, it's up to you, you get to choose
whether to include, whether omit, Yosemite meant killers.

Reading a Biography of Thomas Jefferson in the Months of My Son's Recovery

Because he bought the great swath of mucky swamp
And marshy wetland on the southern edge of the territory,
Then let it alone, so it could fulminate, over time
Into its queer and patchwork, private self—

Because he forged a plowshare from paranoia
About the motivations of Napoleon, declined to incite
A war, and approved, instead, a purchase order—

Because he would have settled for New Orleans, but acquired
The whole thing anyway, through perseverance and hard
Bargaining, and not being too close with the government's
    money—

Because he bought it *all.*
               Half a million acres.
                       Sight unseen—

Because he loved great silences, and alligators, and bustling ports,
And unfettered access to commerce, and international
Trade, and bowery, stone-paved courtyards, noisy
With clattering palms, and formal drawing rooms
Cooled with high ceilings and shuttered windows, furnished
In the lush, upholstered styles of Louis Quinze. Because he valued
Imported wines and dark, brewed coffees, and had a tongue
That understood those subtle differences, but still found himself
Thrilled as a child by the strange, uncatalogued creatures that
    crawled
And swam and winged themselves throughout the native
    Territory—

Because of all this, I return thanks to Thomas Jefferson
For his flawed example of human greatness, for the mind-boggling

Diversity of Louisiana—birthplace of my second son,
13th of December 1990, the largest child delivered
                                        to the state that day . . .

   . . .

Can't help drawing back at how he lived in two minds
Because he was *of two minds* like a person
With old time manic depression: the slaveholder
And the Democrat, the tranquil hilltop of Monticello,
And the ringing cobblestones of Paris, France. The white
Wife, and the black slave mistress . . .

   . . .

Before he was my son, he was contained
Within a clutch of dangling eggs that waited,
All atremble, for his father's transforming glob
Of universal glue.

From the beginning—*before*
The beginning—before he had arranged
Himself into a fetal entity, and begun
To grow inside me, he was endangered
By the mind-breaking molecules our ancestors
Hoarded, and passed forward in a blameless
Game of chance, shuffling the genes.

Even then, two minds circulated inside him,
Tantalizing its brand-new victim with generations
Of charged-up narratives of drugs and drink,
Of suicide and mania, of melancholic unmodulated
Moods, bedeviling distant aunts who died early,
And wild cousins who loved their night drives
On dark roads with no headlights on, speedometer
Straining to the arc of its limit, mothers who danced
On the dining room table, kicking aside the Thanksgiving
Turkey they had carefully basted hours before.

We marveled at him in his bassinette—such
An unsoothable infant, so unreconciled to breathing

Oxygen, wearing a diaper, waiting for milk.
Still small and manageable at first. But whirling
Moods, baby-sized, and effervescent
As the liminal clouds of early spring, stalked him
Even then. Even then

                              This Thing stalked him
Threatening his freedom
                              And his right to self-rule.

   ...

We hold these truths to be self-evident, that all men
are created equal, that they are endowed by their
Creator with certain unalienable Rights, that among
these are Life, Liberty and the pursuit of Happiness.

                              Before we *were*
Ourselves he knew us. Explained us
To ourselves. Gave us a language whereby
We understood the restless grandiosities of our forebears,
And set us off on our well-trod path of personal
Liberty and greedy freedom-seeking. Minted the metaphors
We go on living by and misinterpreting, and clobbering
Over the heads of the rest of the world—Still,
His language stirs me up. Still, I believe
He was a great man, and seek in the painful
Contradictions of his personal life and public
Service, ongoing signs for how to live
In *this* strange era.

   ...

Sometimes it helps to latch on
To someone else's vision
In a crisis—the way I did
At Monticello, so long ago,
Stumbling along the rain-slicked
Bricks of orderly paths. Working-class girl
In cheap shoes and plastic glasses,
Bad teeth. Terrified by the new world

Of the mind I'd entered. From the strict
Arrangements and smoothed-out edges
Of all those interwoven pavers someone baked
From clay, carted there, laid out by hand,
Brick by brick by brick, I carved a small sanity
Where I could rest. And read.

    ...

I know of no safe depository of the ultimate powers
of society but the people themselves. And if we
think them not enlightened enough to exercise
their control with a wholesome discretion,
the remedy is not to take it from them,
but to inform their discretion by education . . .

Once more, we drive our son to the treatment center,
And sign him in, and watch him stripped of identity
And privacy. Shoelaces and cigarettes. Cell phone.
A dog-eared novel by Cormac McCarthy. A plastic bag
Stuffed with things we take away with us, and weep over,
Driving home. He has lost the safe depository of himself.
Is dispossessed. Is lacking any wholesome discretion
On his own behalf. Indicted by genetics, disempowered
By blood, how should we school him, except by love
And psychotropic medications?

    ...

In the long nights when I can't sleep,
When anxiety courses through my body,
Ratcheting up to a stiff rod of fear and dread
I feel impaled upon, I sometimes let my mind
Drift to Thomas Jefferson and his famous
Inconsistencies . . . Here he is
Tranquilly trotting through the bracing sunlight
Of national history, all long bones and red hair,
The eloquent incitements of his discourse scrolling
Out the documents that determined our fate.
But there he is at night, other mind in ascendance,

Tying shut the bed curtains of a lover he inventoried
Among his personal property. With whom he made
Six children. Though he owned her.
And then owned them. His own sons
And Daughters . . .

The way that two things can coexist without
Cancelling each other out—how did he live
Like that? *How does my own son live like that?*
As a schoolchild longs for certainty, I crave
An answer, and sometimes hold my two hands up
To weigh the *yes* against the *no,* slavery
In one hand, freedom in the other: a tiny exercise
In bipolarity that never helps.

    ...

I cannot live without books, he wrote.
And so gave permission for a kind of life
Previously unimaginable: this life I live now—
Soothing myself among my many volumes . . .

What Doesn't Happen

The notion that the carriage wheels clattering through Paris
remind him of the drums from the islands in his father's tales:
clickclack sputterwhir—he could make a song of it, dance
this four-in-hand down the cobbles of the rue du Bac
as he balances his small weight against the pricking cushions
clacksputter whir—all the cadences jumbled together
except the thudding dirge of his heart.

That he can see, in curtained twilight, the violin case in his lap
twitch with every jounce, like an animal trapped under the hunter's
   eye;
that he can sense, down shrouded alleys, danger rustling just as
   surely
as he can feel spring's careless fingers feathering his chest and smell
April's ferment in the stink of the poor marching toward him . . .

Though none of this is true. He hears nothing but clatter.
He can't see the rain-slicked arc of the bridge passing under him
as the pale stone of the palace rears up and he climbs down
to be whisked into the massive *Salle des Machines,*
his father's cloak folded back like a bat's tucked wing—

because it was a dry spring that year on the Continent.

Nonetheless, he ignores his heart's thudding and steps out
onto the flickering stage, deep and treacherous
as a lake still frozen at sunset, aglow with reflected light.
Soon the music will take him across; he'll feel each string's ecstasy
thrum in his head and only then dare to open his eyes to gaze
past the footlights at the rows of powdered curls
(*let's see the toy bear jump his hoops!*)
nodding, lorgnettes poised, not hearing but judging—

except for that tall man on the aisle, with hair
the orange of fading leaves; and the two girls beside him—
one a younger composition of snow and embers,
but the other—oh the other dark, dark yet warm
as the violin's nut-brown sheen . . . miraculous creature
who fastens her solemn black gaze on the boy as if to say
you are what I am, what I yearn to be—

so that he plays only for her and not her keepers;
and when he is finally free to stare back,
applause rippling over the ramparts—even then
she does not smile.

Ungrafted: Jefferson's Vines

You might have considered the root that resisted
drought and mold, that its blander grape would be
better sacrificed to the vine with the fickle bloom,
but a sweeter yield. Not quite invention that would have been,
the manipulation of the garden; if such is flesh,
you would have considered it nonsensical
to the severance. And that would have become the bottle.
What you might have made the candle-flame entered anyway,

the red quickening, evening a slip like a blade
into it. As a dream inheres even into afternoon—
of it, and other—as it dissolves like salt
in broth, like light in water, that was the graft
of what you did with what you might have done—
what might have become the tongue, becoming it.

When I Was a Girl

When I was a girl, climbing outside my
body, every eye I felt, my legs

no longer mine. A circle

of boys, a circle of girls. Let's
play *Slave,* one

said—I'll be *Master,* you can be *Yard
Boss,* you can do

my whipping for me. If I
want the rest to carry me they will

carry me,

they will make a moving throne of
their bodies. This one has

a good set of teeth, I will call her
Nursemaid, she will live in my

mansion, I will
come in the night, *yes,* she will

say, yes. I will write everything out on her
back. When I was

a girl no one kissed me outside of
a word, but the word

couldn't be *kiss,* or *lips,* or *tongue,*
the word had to point to something

outside of us—an ant
carrying a leaf, say—that

was the game. When I was a girl I'd
strap one on, she'd look over her

shoulder, I could make her
smile, I'd whisper, *Find me*

as I'm falling. Scientists

now claim that the ocean is fed by
an invisible ocean, a crystal at

the center of the earth, it waits,

not as vapor, not liquid, not
ice, but crystal, an enormous

jewel, waiting
to open. So much I don't understand. In the

beginning
girls ran across burning fields

with swords made of sticks, girls
hid in trees, stones heavy in their

hands. In the beginning

I was a girl, I held out my hand & it filled with
sunlight. If a bird landed in my palm

I could either crush it
or set it free.

Letter from Poplar Forest

"We abound in the luxury of the peach,"
Jefferson wrote from the sweet heat
of August, 1815, at Poplar Forest in a letter
to his granddaughter, Martha Randolph,

and I think back to the northeast orchards
of my growing up, the dead cherry trees
that kept bearing fruit, the rows
upon rows of apple and pear aligned

as if in West Point drills, the quince
(lone member of their genus) squatting
nearest to the house. There were no almonds
or apricots, of course, as at Monticello.

But a single peach tree somehow, even
as a sapling, bore the gorgeous weight
of full-sized fruit, swells of flesh and juice
unlike other harvests. Of all the bounty bulging

around us, peaches were most coveted,
their fragrance pheromonal: by day
the air was scented with them; at night
my parents sliced them into wine

by candlelight, a sensuous ritual
I was permitted to witness.
If one tree, straining with the weight of its own
fertility, produced such savor, imagine

the abundance of Monticello with its thirty-eight
varietals of peach, their very names a succulence:
Maddalena. Vaga Loggia. Imagine
what that letter conjured for Martha,

for whom, Jefferson wrote, a slave was
at the moment drying peaches in the sun,
as if the undried fruit might overcome
a child; as if that moment could have been

preserved; as if a girl, in the thrall
of such sweet-smelling legacy, might know
what one day she will fling aside—which
pits—and what she will cling to.

Monticello Duet: Outside/In

Memoirs of a Monticello Slave—"a full and faithful account
of Monticello and the family there . . ."

Isaac:

One time Monticello was struck by lightning . . .

    Sally:

    It spills me, granulated, against the walls of caves, (Some place in
        France,

            I can't remember where) enclaves fissured with secrets
                whispered

    in ochre and sepia stolen from the marrowed bones of birds—
        mocking birds winging

            homeward, alight on a dream of Allegheny green.

Isaac:

There was three gates to open,

    the furst bout a mile from the house,

        the other one three quarters;

            then the yard-gate, at the stable

                three hundred yards from the house.

    Isaac had to open the gates.

    Sally:

    I perfect what is dark,

    watch it out, bereft as inhalation, deep across floorboards
        puddled with shadow,

    find the spot our eyes once sought and beg pardon of the water

    for my audacious and parched stare—

Isaac:

The woods and the mountains was often on fire; sometimes I work
    all night

    fighting fire.

Sally:

What was that word and in what language? Can you spell it for
me now,

> *this night, this dark, this sorrow that is not, is not, the word?*

Isaac:

They was forty years at work on that house before Mr. Jefferson
stop building.

> *Sally:*
>
> *The dead still throb with loves and wrongs.*
> *I candle the abyss, remembering its maw,*
> *hands tight-fisted like buds of peonies that refuse to open*
> *in weather hot and then so cold . . .*

Isaac:

Mr. Jefferson had a clock in his kitchen at Monticello; never went
into the kitchen

> except to wind the clock.
>
> *Sally:*
>
> *Where is time? Not a line to be balanced and scaled, but a*
> *whale in the depths of the tale*
> *of this life and this breath, measured in the death of*
> *each next.*

Isaac:

Mrs. Jefferson was small:

> *Sally:*
>
> *His hair was fall air, petaled in words. The windy voice of his*
> *leaves*
> *spoke of shores where he willed us wash the sand and rock the*
> *sands to rocks minuscule . . .*
>
> *Scrubbing so, I erased your etch from his flesh, crossing seas to*
> *where all the trees did not*
> *recall your face.*
>
> *You, sister-mine—porcelain doll—wife, cracked*

mid-breath with death, leaving me with only a tree,
a mango tree, for a friend.

Isaac:

From Monticello, you can see mountains all around as far as the eye
can reach:

see it, raining down this course; sun shining the tops of the hills.

> *Sally:*
> *Human blasphemy is lonely as sleep, each dream a*
> *singular betrayal*
>
> > *beyond translation or love.*

Isaac:

Isaac had to open the gates.

> *Sally:*
> *ummm hmmm.*

[*american verses*, excerpt]

Now excavate the Jeffersonian dry well
in Monticello's yard: the cream ware backfill,

the dishes edged in ceramic feathers, and
the green glass bottles of cherry black

and cranberry black, corn kernels and
the dimpled pits of peaches, and the shards

of mustard pots whose an-hua marks are
(subtle, hidden) (—)

(am I) adorned with a secret wound
that flashes in the catching light ./? I am,
     • • •

in the long, dark throat of the republic,
standing now, the inconceivable result

of the experiment. This dream versus that one.
This is not the first time I have been

half statement, half question ./? Egg and
swirl. Hole and semen. I braid my hair

with three directions. I wash in the kitchen,
wash off the shards

before dropping them into
the dirt's forced mouth

along with the small-eye seeds of sorghum.
The kitchen grows, the sorghum grows

plumes in my sleep. I desire this.
This pleasure of touching faces,

then returning them to the earth,
of making things to future-find.

Or finding ways to keep
a joy. *My* eye on this.

   •••

I will say it "plainly":

Once, out of clouds, Sister told me a story,
but really she was training me to see.

From then, I started
to get good at reading veils.

I was always seeing and getting good
at seeing, but did not learn to really speak.

Or a song begins with air and dies
in air, nearly blue with privacy.

   •••

What codes I smuggled,
were smuggled into me

                                  ?

Irreconcilable Greenness of
the Body's Blood Before Air,

tell me we are the relations of the leaves!?
But you come out dressed

in the secret leaping of names!:
staghorn, pequin, cochineal, red wing.

The first foxes of my childhood
thrown deadly across the back of a couch

from where they gawked
and warned.

   •••

At thirteen, when I first bled, came
the knowledges:

in the domestic space of the laundry room,
to the work, work of the washer and dryer,

surrounded by hangers and sheets and clothes,
my mother warned me of everything. This is my fear,

This is my fear, This is my fear,
This is my fear, she said.

And later, my almond-skinned brother
heading to work after dark in a once-burning city,

with other browns and beautifully darkskinned
friends who were also boys and almost-men,

over the telephone, This is my fear, This is my fear,
This is my fear, she said,

for she loved us, and warning was
what she knew, in this country, loving should be.

   • • •

In 1771, part of me is here and part of me
still coming: this, the body's best trick.

Already, one grandfather is laying the tracks
and one grandmother is picking coffee, and

one has not even heard, yet, this word "America."
To think I thought I knew nothing,

could say nothing about "America,"
so silently was I jennied into the country's spool.

Yes, I still believe in the grass,
but the truer story's hidden

in the hair and air, the eyes of trees,
the dark hours of the worms

in the mountain,
the dream of the one beneath

The Dreaming
One.

Not just what we wanted to be,
but what we kept versus what we buried,

underground versus
above the ground.

You know,
Jefferson versus Jefferson?

A series of pivots
and hidden marks and things.

This defining itself
                        against
                                    that. That's all.
    . . .
In second grade, Teacher chose me to be
Betsy Ross. In a classroom play,

I pretended to stitch the flag, for example,
while wearing a bonnet on my head.

The fall was turning things yellow.
I was sitting in a room near the edge

of a continent. The years rode redly
through my hot face: the dread of

that foolishness, even then.
She was white and I was black and

even then I knew that I, in a bonnet,
meant something else:

How could I be Betsy Ross?
How could I be Betsy Ross?

When, mostly, then, I
was in the yard, or

had yet to see the majesty
of these purple mountains.

Except, of course, here
this is also always true:

"Blood" of conjunctions,
History of conjunctions:

and this, *but* this,
yet this, *so* this.

And I, here,
among "them."

> *The title and last line of the poem mean to reference Robert Hayden's
> "[American Journal]."*

Monticello

My grandfather would give me coins
fished from stained denim pockets
when I pestered him enough, or looked glum
to the point of pity. Go buy some comic books,
he instructed, but I feared
he'd one day ask for cigarettes
or wine or one of the skin mags
that were sold beside *Richie Rich* and *Iron Man*,
and to my ten years were
terrifying. He'd quiz me:
what did *anno domini* mean?
What did *VJ Day* stand for?
What was on the backs of nickels
(Jefferson's Monticello,
little hill in Italian,
then not much more than architectural trivia)?
Now I see each morning
walking in to work
its white roof throwing off sunlight.
When he died last year,
unable to speak following two strokes,
I didn't attend his funeral
ten hours away. I imagined
the day was somber,
lustrous with rain,
appropriately mournful.
A few wept and made romantic noise.
I imagined I could tell him
how close I live
to Monticello, though this
proximity has led me to visit just once,

in autumn, as leaves
fall away and the air turns to cool rain.
I didn't stay long:
I imagined the damage
my wheelchair
would cause if I spasmed,
if my feet crashed
through the double glass doors of the study,
if I punched a hole
in the wall's thick plaster.
I left and it was dark
outside and below us
glowing ribbons wound into town.
That night, the stars,
this poem like apology.

Monticello

    Snow is falling
on the age of reason, on Tom Jefferson's
    little hill & on the age of sensibility.

    Jane Austen isn't walking in the park,
she considers that this gray crust
    of an horizon will not do;
she is by the fire, reading William Cowper,
    and Jefferson, if he isn't dead,
has gone down to K-Mart
    to browse among the gadgets:
    pulleys, levers, the separation of powers.

I try to think of history: the mammoth
    jawbone in the entry hall,
Napoleon in marble,
    Meriwether Lewis dead at Grinder's Trace.

    I don't want the powers separated,
one wing for Governor Randolph when he comes,
    the other wing for love,
                    private places
    in the public weal
    that ache against the teeth like ice.

    Outside this monument, the snow
catches, star-shaped,
    in the vaginal leaves of old magnolias.

A Poem Inspired by a Frederick Douglass Middle Schooler's Essay on Thomas Jefferson

would have been written[1] except on the way to the library
the boy who'd pulled the name of the third president
from Mrs. Getwell's makeshift top hat of presidential topics[2]
stopped to watch a homeless brother named Red
beat his bird-chest to keep beat as he sang about bling
(though it sounded to the boy like *being*) into the barred
entrance of a vacuous parking garage for echo while being
videotaped[3] so that it could be viewed somewhere sometime
in the future by us,[4] after which the boy returned home[5]
and that night dreamed Jefferson (who was the root
of his troubles) explained to every soul[6] between the Founding
Fathers (though it sounded like *Con*founding—LOL—to the boy)
and Mrs. Getwell's Frederick Douglass Middle School class
how we[7] are the root of our troubles, until in the dream
the boy confronted (though it sounded like *comforted*) Red
(who as you can see looks a lot like Thomas Jefferson!)
saying, if you're scared, talk to a friend or family member right
before bed. Sometimes it helps to talk to someone about your fear. [8]

[1] (Among the blacks is misery enough, God knows, but no poetry.[TJ])

[2] You may be capable of imagining the possible inevitable title of
this particular essay is "Some Fish" but you will be incapable of deciding
whether it is about some fish or *how* some fish and whether fish are a
metaphor for blacks or *some* blacks.

[3] https://www.youtube.com/watch?v=FOHFOCbnLDo

[4] Imagine "us" stands for useful service, ugly servant, unusual
sentiment, unctuous smiles, uncle sambo, utter shame, under summons,
unified simplicity, upper spine, urgent slither, umbical spell, utility shout,
and universal sadness.

[5] Imagine you are under 12, born to a wealth of cousins and aunts in a
midcentury mirage; imagine the edges of your look are fraying, the body
resisting and filling with change and color covering the soul like a veil
covering the soul.

⁶ Dear Importations, Provocations, Convulsions, Secretions and Objections residing in the membranes and colors of the blood: to justify a general conclusion, requires many observations, even where the subject may be submitted to the anatomical knife, to optical glasses, to analysis by fire or by solvents.^{TJ} Our most presidential subject goes into the ground and three pink peonies sprout from the grave. (What further is to be done with them?)

⁷ Today I am—

Is it really that they have less hair on the face and body, that they require less sleep, is it really that they are ardent after their females, that their grievances are transient, they are dull, tasteless, and anomalous? Such are the questions the boy planned to research and address to the apocryphal third president as well as his dear Saint George Tucker, dear Countrymen, and dear King Rufus King. (By "they" I mean "us.")

⁸ To overcome your fear of color you must determine the triggers for your fear and consider removing caffeine from your diet.

Near the Rim of the Ideal

     My anarchist & i   fly home   from the east
in sight of the rim   of the ideal — —;

                            on the right
   the least moon drops   — — a vitamin
b,   simple, pink, mechanical . . .
ellipses on the wing   in seamless   patches . . . . . .
         nails by Boeing—
    this week,   the horror   in Gaza,   in Ukraine,
        a plane shot down — — the concept of *nation*
stalls in the bitter brain (bitter brain bitter brain
bitter brain . . .)

We've been asked to think   about Jefferson —uh—ohoh
    founding fathers   — — the founding
           words search for   their roots
    in air — — *federal* [*"Why are you making
such a big
       federal case over it . . ."*] *federal* from *bheidh,*
              meaning: faithful; *fiancé*
    also comes from this . . .
          What are we faithful to?   love's   mystery
at the rim   of the ideal . . . color between
 shapes . . . Monticello's columns   are faithful
    to the porch — —   they look like:

           @ @ @ @   @ @ @ @
           really do   **really do**

           really do   **really do**

           really do   **really do**

& the copula— — not stopped   by beauty or distress—
        Doric— —   enlightened thought,

faithful   to space,
& space   is faithful to the circular — —

          Deists liked their God   absent & elegant
          . . . . . . independent God,   a rationalist—
where is He   hiding?   maybe that's little Him   near
      the wing,   floating,   neutral
in   neutral mist,
          far from Jefferson's house — — now,   why
                         did he think he deserved all that?
      slave houses & smoke houses,
          the dustless silks,   the clock   he designed
          with his mind, with his mind   — —
patrician rocking chair   called for by   natural law . . .

          My anarchist & i, we could love such   law
      as long as it's   the law of the rock & dirt   not
          my country 'tis of trading   metals & cloth
                         carried on the backs of children — —
          not   mastery over
   bog turtle & purple bean,
pale mucket,   & sneeze weed,   *nnnot* mastery over vetch,
      mastery over independence   as in
   we sold these truths   to be self-evident as in
          Mileage Plus from Chase, zero percent intro annual
                    fee for the first year
then $95 after that
not mastery   because skies are friendly,   mastery
      over water because the slide   inflates automatically— —

my anarchist & i declare   dependence
          on the invisible,
                    & on its runt   the visible . . .
          not to hold   these truths   to be self- evident
if specifics fail . . .
 Now far   far down   in Jefferson's garden — — in
rungs   & rungs of fixed dirt   the united snakes &

embryonic   spirits   push breath
        into   pollen puffs   above
finely ridged   carrots & onions \/\/\/\/\/\/\
      connecting the ideal   through their roots   — —
pushing miraculous periscopes   out of earth,
past the fungal layer   of powdery nonDeist   soil,
        quite dependent spirits all over the place   — —
we hear   he tended it himself . . .
            O Jefferson, paradox,   finest of men
      who wound down like his clock. . . . Slaves

remained & he was neutral as god
& he was neutral as god
he was neutral as god
was neutral as god
neutral as god
as god

            We, the difficult   daughters
hold these truths to be   selflessly   evident
          as   microbes on   our nationless eyelids
      await   the arrival of the sun—

Nora's Nickel

She gave it to me with a little story
about a coin like this one dropped through floorboards
where she lived as a girl in Mississippi.
The nickel that she lost had a Red Indian
instead of her favorite president for heads
and where the one she gave me had a house
for tails hers had a buffalo. What's more
beneath her house, like many in Mississippi,
the pigs and chickens nosed and pecked for food.
A pig unearthed her Indian-head nickel
and so she gave it as a Sunday offering
for foreign missions. Wasn't that pig clever
(and every gift of a nickel came with this question)
to root a nickel all the way to China?

Grandmother Nora on her hilltop in San Diego
with the boulevards arrayed in all directions
like fields of sunny, cottony concrete,
with her Pall Malls and white-wigged figurines,
with her okra simmering through the afternoon,
with her professed love of all her Mexican friends
like the grocer's boy who came to her back door,
was all I knew of the South when I was a child
and we both lived in Southern California.
The house she'd grown up in in Mississippi
I pictured as looking like the house on the nickel,
with cracks in the floor where all the money you lost
could find its way to children in far off countries
and help to pay the way to San Diego.

Incognitum

In the Indian Hall the skeletons assemble, buried
trade beads brought to light gleam like ruin
run glamorous alluvium: evidence of someone
else's way through valleys dense, interior, and distant.

I want for hands in ocher, for one whose hands
once held my own. I learn to long for thought
arising through the floor of my mind, a song alone
in sound recessing into the small noise of my breath.

The tongue turns awry—*it may be asked, why I*
Insert the mammoth, as if it still existed? I ask in return why I
Should omit it, as if it did not exist?—I am little more
than a string figure, one of a divided couple danced

into a seam of time. At the margin of our desolation
relics so old bear no odor. *He may well exist there now,*
as he did formerly where we find his bones. The eye of a storm
stares inward: we are fallen together for excavation.

Jefferson's Daughters

Snow is falling
on the age of reason, on Tom Jefferson's
    little hill & on the age of sensibility.
—Robert Hass, "Monticello"

And it's drafty in his house of enlightenment
with its many windows on the wilderness
    and its domed oculus an unblinkered eye on high,
where his daughters who have been to Paris

    cannot travel to Richmond for a dance—
their phaeton's skeleton too delicate
    for the rutted roads blue with snow and shade—
they, who have walked the halls of Palladio

    and watched North America—Virginia, really,
its shores salted with tobacco and slavery,
    scrub pine and salt back, recede
behind a scalloped wall of waves

    like an immigrant's dream in reverse,
borne back into the dark folds of France's catholic habits,
    where Maria, the image of her long-dead mother
and namesake of the Virgin Mother herself,

    wanted to convert—well, here they are
nearly cloistered at nineteen, snowbound
    in their father's great georgic experiment
while the social season whirls without them,

    and the sisters grow spiny as fiddlehead ferns,
their foreheads pressed to the plate-glass walls,
    truer terrarium than house these days.
So early they look to the windows to find

the thin ghosts of themselves staring back.
Their quick steps on the stairs,
    a ladder jackknifed and narrow,
are minced as minuets they turn in time

    to the tinny cymbal of the gong
which rings in house and field alike.
    Do not pity them this,
slighted by American abstraction,

    freedom for a few and all that.
Know that if there are locks in the house
    (and there are)
they at least hold the key

    as mistress over all but mostly larder and cellar,
where the tongues of bells clang incessantly,
    their days wound tight as the Great Clock itself.
Oh, if there is a god here,

    he enters the kitchen weekly
to wind the hands and let it go.
    Maria and Martha travel whole days
on the tethered length of needle and thread.

    They embroider miles in the stitching
and backstitching of a cushion,
    and perhaps they are content
in their kingdom of two.

    Someone, after all, has to dust the jawbone of history
in the entrance hall—that curiosity cabinet
    of the continent, contained and arrayed:
map, mineral, & mastodon,

    proof of a past they can only imagine
and evidence of the land where they live
    but barely see—
their horizon clipped by cloud and privilege.

Poised as they are on the cusp of the country,
practically curtsying on the precipice of wilderness,
    they stay indoors instead to watch
the antlers in the front hall branch and grow

    on walls by candlelight
and the clock's cannonball plummet
    into the dark understory until
first light drags another weight,

    groaning, into dawn when they must rise,
as their absent father bid them be
    alert to survey his *workhorse of nature,*
the terraced gardens iced as wedding cake.

    There is always work waiting to be done.
Men and women, dutiful as dumbwaiters,
    ferry water and wood.
Outside the monument snow falls on

    the shallow pond with its fish locked in ice
and the fox curled in his dark den of desire,
    dreaming of spring, for the age of reason
to finally see the light.

    In the ornamental forest of the grove,
the seedpods of magnolias are packed tight.
    The old dominion drowses half-asleep,
the fist of her buds less blossom than bomb.

Daddy Hemmings Was Good with Curves

Whether a sled, toy, cabinet, desk,
    or Jefferson's landau carriage,
        a hundred times he grafted cherry

& mahogany, almost as one, true
    to wit & wheels firmly shaped
        on a notion, this prime joiner

could square a circle sighting a line
    straight down a taut stretch
        of twine held by two nails.

Go slow, be patient as the Maker
    on the third day, he thought
        when facing the puzzle of a job.

Blueprint or not, the plantation knew
    he was a man who betted his life
        against the seasons in wood.

Did he use the words love & kin
    when he asked permission
        to marry his beloved Priscilla?

He knew the names & bloodlines
    running clear through Monticello,
        around tree-lined paths & hills

surrounding laconic whispers
    of station & contracts. At first,
        an out-carpenter, he cut trees,

raised barns, hewed logs, & helped
    build Mulberry Row where songs
        of Ireland & Africa dovetailed

& he learnt the law of every plane,
    the slant & set of honed blades,
        the curlicues of dust rising

in the morning light, the haft
    driven by his hands. His sweat
        from age fourteen was in wood

held together by pegs & horse glue,
    as well as a hundred other cuts
        perfectly tongued & grooved

as flesh. He had measured up
    a slab of black walnut to save
        in the attic for his master's coffin

before cutting off enough for
    a child's sewing table, working
        the saw with & against the grain.

Epiphanies

I was thinking about epiphanies
and how the nowhere they come from
isn't a nowhere here on earth,
but like a nowhere in the fourth
dimension. I forget how many
dimensions they say we have these days.
An epiphany just pops into
your brain and suddenly something
you never thought about before
becomes a big sensation, and most
of the time it makes you glad because
you've got some special insight now,
as if there's a magnitude of knowledge
that's hidden from ordinary life.
It's like a butterfly is flying
around in a garden in your brain.
It's nice to have an epiphany.
I wonder if they have dimensions
in Heaven? And consider this—
do they need epiphanies in Heaven?
Probably not, if Heaven is what
they say it is—illumination,
and everything revealed, and bliss.
I also think epiphanies
are quiet, like looking at a field
at night and how it's darker than
the sky and the fireflies float
so calmly blinking on and off.
It's beautiful to see a field
like that, alive in all dimensions.
I wonder if Thomas Jefferson

ever cuddled Sally and watched
the fireflies dazzle a field
at Monticello? He had ideas,
some good ones, I think, but he was so
enlightened he probably thought he had
enough enlightenment. That's why
I really doubt if Jefferson
ever had an epiphany.
He probably noted the fireflies
and recorded the date when they appeared
from year to year, and maybe a night
when they seemed to be more numerous,
but no epiphanies for him—
he wanted things to be just so.
Call me un-American,
but really rational people believe
everything can be explained;
they get so carried away with being
rational they can't imagine
an epiphany. It's like the fourth
dimension doesn't exist for them.
They have no idea what they've missed.
It's kind of an epiphany
to think some people never have them,
it's kind of a mini-epiphany.
I can tell my ordinary life
is changed by imagining a night
at Monticello in the summer
and the different kinds of night there were
and the absence of epiphanies,
despite the glories of that place.

On Hearing the Waterthrush Again, Jefferson

March 1794

ordered a Nebbiolo, briskmost vintage,
to be fetched from the cellar;
        ordered Lilly, their overseer,

to deliver the canal men
an extra whiskey ration by
        the same cart, mule-drawn, that hauled

the grindstone, spare tools. See,
the dogwood petals were beginning
        to drop, and hickory's fires flared dusk

wilder than the day's measures
of rain, last storm a gusty pelting
        around five, followed by blue

in breaks like waking. Walking,
he'd heard parula, cardinal, spooked
        a blue winged teal (pale whorl of its face),

countless geese, turtles, a green heron,
wood ducks in pairs. *My fits of head-ache*
        that dawn he'd inked *have stuck some days*

5. hours. Stingers, still. Yes, everything reeked
of abundance, the strafe & groan beneath
        all growth, banks a forge where blossoms

were sparks rising from that hammer
no hand ever bears. Even the river—
        siltslappy Rivanna—seemed to have grown

wings, a throat lusty and coarse. He heard
molt. Heard vowels, their origins, too,
        but knew only the lost could follow such

speech, if speech, and turned for home.

Symmetry

A rational man, he recognized the beauty in balance.
He sketched the classical temples, Palladio's plans.

For Monticello he built one wing, and later the other,
a matching pavilion at the end of each.

For the Renaissance house between them, he drew
a circle in a square, its arc indicating a home.

He wrote a dialog between the head and the heart—
a balancing act that the heart couldn't tip.

In his right hand, the broil of making a nation,
the thick of politics to keep it going.

In his left, the decades of building a farm—
his refuge, his solace among mountains.

Jefferson would separate the Church from the State,
the time for action and the time for thought.

Mornings for letters, horseback at noon.
Who worked in the wings. Who lived under the dome.

Monticello

for Lisa Russ Spaar

We climbed the steep hidden stairway
to Jefferson's "brain," the octagon
floating at the top of the house, clear

panes, round as eyes, Mars yellow walls.
Sunlight on a green floor, up there, where
the Docent let us go. You thought you could

see what he once saw: ". . . sublime to look
down into the workhouse of Nature, to see
her clouds, hail, snow, rain, thunder, all

fabricated at our feet . . ." just past the roofs
of the slave quarters below. Below the dome,
more natural fabrication, the house ticking as

the Great Clock worked, the windplate weather-
vane spun up dumbwaiters, pivoting swing doors,
the multiple pens of the "copying machine," this

power house running daily on beautifully forged chains.
A brain that invented America, imagining its opposite,
the pens copying out possibilities of tyranny. What he

saw from the top of the house, the steep flight into our
cyber-world, an inter-net of human nature, noble, vile.
He saw it when he descended the steps, hearing cruel gossip.

Said he'd "get a machine for scolding invented," get
a machine to be cruel. "Because it is a business not fit
for any human heart." That America, ongoing, invented,

we looked out at it that day, up at the top of his house.

To Avoid Thinking of Betsy Walker Reclining in a Bedroom at John Coles's Plantation, Thomas Jefferson Imagines the Orchard at Monticello,

composing, in his mind, a note to Antonio about peach trees:
graft the Balyals where indifferent peaches have failed.
And please remember to fill the apple orchard
on the North side of the rolling mountain
so the accumulation of leaves will flourish in rows
winding on a level round the hill.
He liked to imagine, for this promiscuous moment,
the apple trees' petals sprung to abandon their trees,
like a woman's hair loosened in the air
above the manageable grid of his fruitery.
The terraced vineyards hold heavy grapes,
obedient in cultivation
having taken to structure for their scandent vines,
and climbed there, wandering.

A trailing habit is robust; it must not be left alone,
it must not exceed a border. Without design,
the fruit trees will increase and overrun,
burst out their boundaries, and ruin everything.
Of the troubled English gardens he had written:
too much evergreen. Clipt yews grown wild.
Shyness must be managed too. At Coles's plantation,
he had faked a headache and left the gentlemen,
crept among the halls and found her darkening room.
She would be undressing or in bed, bare
beneath her shift's linen borders. Wander beyond there
he could not. She did raise her voice against him.
But still, earlier in the day,
to have placed that note in her hand,

to have grafted desire on the paper and slipped it
beneath the cuff of her sleeve. Under the wrist
(he'd note a raspberry color) she was flush with blood runners,
a fruitish blush undoing the entire economy.
He should measure the vigor of his manhood
and note it in a secret book. He should note the tenure
of the full showing as it pressed
(privately but beautifully) against his own disturbing breeches.
And back down the hall he went, secret and untamed.

The contradiction is not lost on him.
To reduce the wilds to their managed, domestic state
then decorate by innovation and design,
his hand on every beautiful, complicated thing
under clouds that seem to have the old gods in them,
inflicting tortures, pouring libations and laughing.

from Thomas Jefferson

XV

My harpsichord
my alabaster vase
and bridle bit
bound for Alexandria
Virginia

The good sea weather
of retirement
The drift and suck
and die-down of life
but there is land

XVI

These were my passions:
Monticello and the villa-temples
I passed on to carpenters
bricklayers what I knew

and to an Italian sculptor
how to turn a volute
on a pillar

You may approach the campus rotunda
from lower to upper terrace
Cicero had levels

XVII

John Adams' eyes
      dimming
Tom Jefferson's rheumatism
           cantering

XVIII

Ah soon must Monticello be lost
                    to debts
  and Jefferson himself

                              to death

XIX

Mind leaving, let body leave
Let dome live, spherical dome
and colonnade

Martha (Patsy) stay
"The Committee of Safety
must be warned"

Stay youth—Anne and Ellen
all my books, the bantams
and seeds of the senega root

Green-Winged Teals

Letter from Lewis among the Mandans, March 1805

Even before the last snows have disappeared
they're back, their fiery heads and brilliant green eye patches
skimming low over the water, dabbling again in the cattails and
    reeds,

rarely dipping all the way under for food, as they rarely did before,
restless, returned from some distant, different stand
of weeds—maybe below you, along the Rivanna—another river
    they need no name for.

Freedom and the Lie: Monticello and Thomas Jefferson: Plan

Freedom. Land. Water. Plants. Air. Mother Earth.
Freedom. Body. Food. Growth. Earth Mother.

Word as rhetoric is easy. Enough. Too easy.
Really. Intellect and the land—that's where the test is.
Thomas Jefferson never begged for water. Never argued
for it. Never thanked Indigenous People. I'm sure.

Freedom is a mind set. It is plan: sought and decided.
Not negotiated. Jefferson was law. Plan. According to him
and God, air was his. Plan. Therefore Monticello had no need
for justification at all. Plan. With no permission. Nor obligation.

Freedom is never its own. Monticello constructed.
Simple as fact and act. Indigenous People and Mother Earth died.
Freedom's constructions stand and will stand as law stands.
Until the lie-law undermines undermines undermines its own.

Written in collaboration with Jami Proctor-Xu

Axis Mundi

There's a spinach with a prickly seed I like
to grow beside the Bloomsdale in the heat
of our Virginia spring. It's not as sweet
as you might want a green to be, but will spike

a salad half-way into June just fine.
It is one of the things I always try to grow
that also grew and grows at Monticello,
the little mountain of slaves and nails and wine

that Jefferson planted about an hour north
of here and carpeted in orach and lilac,
cardoon, mache, sesame, linden, and sumac,
all of it in the wind blown back and forth.

I won't lie—I plant the spinach only because
it's another idea that works. It's not darker or later
than the Bloomsdale or somehow subtly greater.
I've learned there is a wormhole in the laws

of growing food: you'll always find some way
to relearn what you've spent time learning; a man
whose body is free can find himself again
at home with chains. I try my best to sway

the wind and sun and rain, but really just switch
what they will fall on. At least I can still watch
things grow—it seems significant, the patch
of forwardest peas, the sunchokes, and the spinach,

its first long not-true leaves, for what it's worth,
like the wide stretch of arms, the grasping hands,
of the smallest greenest imaginable man
pulling himself at last up out of the earth.

from Mulattress

I want to talk about your house, how *they've*
painted it "oyster white." As if home were a pearl *secret*ed
about the sand-grain of your bed. You speak *less by*
the declarations of the body (*the kidneys*
& the red-gold gallop of your tongue) *& more*
by your French partitioned doors. When I walk *by the*
library, even your chair turns its spine. My fabulous *glands*
weep a little, under the arms. Strange how the cabinet *of the skin*
you hardly registered, until you did. *Which gives*
me such a headwound. When I think of all *them*
crystal tumblers nobody'll ever use again, *a very strong*
loneliness takes me up. You're so sharp *& disagreeable*
to hold. *Je t'adore.*

Monticello Vase

In the Monticello I have never visited,
no two rooms sit at the same height: to walk
here is to be continually off your footing,
each sunken room radiating out from its squat
rotunda like a series of thoughts nursed
by strangers: this one with its homemade
polygraph and whalebone walking stick; that
with its rose-trellis wallpaper; one room filled
with women's portraits; another empty,
white, severe. Past the imposing
entrance with its chieftain's tomahawks
and revolutionary campaign paintings
his private quarters lie. Here
are cabinets of French faience
and Waterford ink wells, a wine cellar full
of Madeira. In the library, someone cropped
the painted mural of moose and mule deer
large enough to stun Buffon had he seen them:
the American animal being more robust,
as the president once declared,
than those shriveled European creatures
stunted from living on royal grounds.
It sits beside a map of land
rich enough to feed the cotton
acres his in-laws cultivated, the map itself
preserved under glass beside some lacework
made by his wife Martha's house slave,
Critta, with which the estate
could not bear to part. Upstairs,
a red and white "Wedding Rings" quilt
on the bed of Polly, his daughter,

who liked to sketch her father's face
on packets of *belles lettres,* his blunt head
faded to sepia, as has the thick hair,
once fox-red, in his hallway
Trumbull portrait. His own bedroom
contains only a globe and orrery for ornament,
a formal desk with its swiveling chair
that he invented, a dumbwaiter
installed in one corner suggesting a mind
both ingenious and practical,
though it was this taste for hidden
spaces, chutes, and secret rooms
that has nearly hollowed out the building's
foundation. Off the kitchen—small, octagonal,
so warm it feels like entering
the heart—lies the smallest of these rooms.
It contains a single table
on which a glass vase sits. If I looked
closely at it, the faint shapes
of mangled buffalo might appear,
ribs upthrust through piles of flesh
etched into the base ring of the glass.
A dozen interlocking hooves and horns
twisted together to form great chains
or waves, bodies linked together by the leg,
a wolf between them snapping at a man
who grips him by the ears.
The vase commemorates the nation's
Corps of Discovery: the scene itself culled
from Lewis's journal's descriptions
of the Indian jump he found the winter
before he lost his mind.
Above the vase, a yellowed lithograph
of the aged president rests, a piece
of scratched glass covering it: the gray eyes

seeming to shift up and away
from his viewer's stare.
The vase's color at its lip
is something between burnt wheat
and burnished copper. It has a sheen
like the painted flanks on the portrait
of Jefferson's favorite horse, Caractacus:
a powerful charger, named for the Saxon king
who fought the Romans, was taken as their slave
but spoke so eloquently he was given
his freedom. A model for Americans
to revere, the president wrote, even if they do not
remember him, symbol of native cunning
and resistance, whose power lies
in reported speeches.

Heirloom

Monticello

Over every confidence, something arches.
A bower, as anyone might know.

What was wondered is now dropped—a stitch—
Or set down, as on a tray, and carried away.

And in the crook of the branch, a message:
I myself have lived in secret.

Some days the sky whitens, but does not absolve.
There is no cure but time, and for time, no cure.

Thus, among the beauties, grief, also,
Itself an heirloom, held up, handed down.

History begins to come true as we tell it.
This is the spot where.

Asylum from Grief, September 1795

After "A Dialogue between the Head and the Heart"

You found it in my bosom—
fancied her father's features in my face,
retraced the whole series of your fondness
on my two-shades too brown skin.

You were a diplomat of bedroom politics,
kept your promise to never wed again. Still
flesh you hungered—flesh you found but
couldn't have from women meant for other men.

I was sixteen when you found the inside of my body,
made it an asylum for your grief. I am the angel
reincarnate, *the bait of pleasure—no hook beneath me.*
My body now blooming—bearing a body

one shade closer to the one you mourned,
one shade closer to a world that is yours.

Thomas Jefferson in Kathmandu

Experience hath shewn, that even under the best forms of government, those entrusted with power have, in time, and by slow operations, perverted it into tyranny.

—Thomas Jefferson, *Preamble to a Bill for the More General Diffusion of Knowledge* (1778)

Packed in Thamel into a beat-up Tempo, that minivan
    which serves as public transportation in Nepal,
        I'm thumbing your visage on a nickel near the tan

faces of seekers and trekkers, the various people
    of foreign descent who throng the dusty road
        in saffron shirts and rudraksha malas, the steeple

up ahead really a stupa where we stop to unload
    passengers and accept others. Here, I think of you
        TJ, in the faux–Gilbert Stuart portrait that stood

smelling of agar from petri dishes plus an old gym shoe
    odor that never seemed to dissipate from the halls
        of my high school named for you where I went through

facial hair, trigonometry, punk rock, soccer balls,
    SATs, angst, in short the whole gamut of adolescent
        failure and triumph. Now, standing in front of stalls

selling Himalayan masks, frozen in poses of pent-
    up animal rage and wood-carved rictuses of wrath,
        I remember how many long hours I once had spent

under your unnoticed gaze, working on some math
    problem or pining over the redhead I was smitten
        with, carrying my dog-eared copy of Sylvia Plath,

dreaming myself a writer before I had even written
    a stanza worth rereading. It would be much later
        at the University you built where I'd be bitten

by the bug properly, a sensation made ever greater
    in the walks I would take traversing your serpentine
        walls, alone, at home in my own mind the way a crater

gives shape to a surface by suggesting what's unseen,
    what might have been once, still what is yet to come.
        I traced the rim of my own unknowing, still so green

but ambitious, questioning everything, trying to shun
    nothing, striking together stones to try to make a fire
        that would burn brighter and deeper than a twinning sun.

Here now is Chitipathi the skeletal lord of the Funeral Pyre
    and Mahakala, the great black one, personal tutelary
        of Kubla Khan, with flared nostrils, bared fangs and ire

to spare. And here you are on your plantation, Mulberry
    Row, where slaves worked as smiths, joiners, weavers,
        carpenters, and hostlers, each of whom has a story

untold on unmarked graves or in your writings. Grievers
    mourned your death on Independence Day but of them,
        what? Here I am in Alderman Library working levers

of the elevator moving in half-floors slow as phlegm
    seeping down a basin drain. Here you are in Paris wearing
        yarn stockings, velveteen breaches, the exquisite hem

of your waistcoat like wild honeysuckle baring
    subtle blossoms. Here are all the dark bodies going
        into ground after a lifetime of labor and you staring

from Mount Rushmore, me from under the flowing
    rim of the Annapurna mountains. Here is the Bill
        of Rights, where Sally Hemings does her light sewing.

I'm on the other side of the world and still
      can't see clearly what has succeeded and what failed
            in the grand American experiment. I eat my fill,

no prayer bowl to beg from, yet have been jailed
      and bailed out, slurred, even refused service at a diner
            250 years after you were born. I know I'm not nailed

to a cross, but why is it that I feel so much finer
      and more contented in a country ruled by Maoists
            and Marxists than I do in the democratic, designer

shining city on the hill where all the Taoists,
      Hindus, and Buddhists I'm meeting want to move
            to regardless, *to start new lives in the USA*? How is it

possible that the Newari dancers' ancient groove
      feels more timely than twerking, that I'd rather eat
            dosas and dal than haute cuisine? No need to prove

an answer to those questions as they're mine to read
      and puzzle out, but grown from a seed planted
            at your plantation into a towering crop I now need

heed. Democracy is a fine ideal yet to be supplanted,
      but does it coexist with capitalism? Today I was told
            a Nepalese proverb which might be loosely translated

as "cumin in an elephant's mouth," meaning how all gold
      shines valueless next to our own nothingness, how the priceless
            figs we hunger for are impossible to be bought or sold.

I've secreted the nickel now into the folds of a torn dress
      a woman with child uses to collect rupees. She is our
            mother from another life and you and I are no less,

no more than brothers. If even in this late hour,
      honesty is the first chapter in the book of wisdom,
            then its epilogue must be compassion. Not power.

Cut-and-Paste Republic

With a razor's edge, to pare away the *artificial*
vestments until the original man is revealed.

A pot of glue and a brush of hog bristle,
to piece together the greatest tale ever told,

which is the story of himself, savoring a glass
of wine from his own vineyard, knowing

such juices are derived from downpours
but that no water may be wished into wine

and no cripple may rise to prune the vines
nor a blind man to admire such a tawny tint.

This is not to deny the holy spirit, nor heaven,
nor even the tale of the Great Flood and Ark

 (in a similar disaster, Carolinians rescued
livestock and dogs)—however, to arrive

at *pure principles* one must siphon off
all *essences and emanations,* or to be blunt,

all *nonsense,* until a *sublime and benevolent code*
be as evident as his hands, *two simple*

evangelists splicing the salutary inspirations,
just as states are joined in perfect bonds,

and as the noble parts of a man combine
in felicitous acts, as when Jefferson's blade

cuts away the cleansing of lepers, the miraculous
catch of fish, the calming of the tempest.

For now, in the space where Jesus was crucified,
there is a garden and abundant grapes,

and the rolling of a stone to seal his sepulcher
is more resonant than a resurrection

to the man who exclaims *I am of a sect
by myself, as far as I know.*

Mr. Jefferson Speaks of Rapture

Natural Bridge, Virginia

Even though he knows Cedar Creek
pours through it, he wants to believe
it was cloven by a great convulsion.
Master of all he surveys, he's
been measuring it from below for some time. This,
he will say, must not be
pretermitted. God's Roman arch,
he will not say, not this empire hater. He always
provides a number of numbers.

The arch approaches
the semi-elliptical form; but the larger axis
of the ellipsis, which would be the cord
of the arch, is many times longer than the transverse.

He will write that *few men have resolution*
to . . . look over into the abyss. He fell
on his hands and knees at the edge.
Intolerable! he cried, his head cloven
by a savage migraine . . .

Back at his desk, he writes
of *so beautiful an arch, so elevated, so light,*
and springing
as it were up to heaven.

He likes the word *sublime.*
But he can't get out of his head
the creeping and peeping.

Mr. Jefferson writes through the night.

Scuppernongs

Dusk in Monticello's autumn arbor—
the squire reaches into wasp-haunted
leaves to touch a single native grape
more treasured than *Muscat blanc,* catawba,
or *lacrimi dolci.* Seizing the evening,

he strolls the slate maze and terrace alone
to remember his late wife and lament
the decade he's struggled in vain to mate
the Old World delicates to *Vitus
vulpina,* the fragrant grape Aesop's fox

would have said anything just to taste.
"The homely scuppernong," he thinks, "is
dusky, Southern, its ruminant juices rife
with a sweetness indigenous to any
Edenic muscadine tribe, yet immune

to local perils like the aphid, black rot,
powdery mildew, fretters." He moves
through spider floss and spike dandelions.
"Unrefined," he judges, "but with vigor,"
and yearns to wed the spirits of a neighbor's

lowbrow tendrils to the courtesies
of Europe—nuance, dry insinuation,
a widower's oblique ardor. Ruminant
himself, graying russet, Jefferson maintains
a sovereign's posture and is stepping

in dew now through the garden pavilion
to spy the Marseilles fig espaliered,
limbs twisted, crucified. A spilling fountain

silvers. Late birds trill. Sunset is polished
with jeweler's rouge, a French touch. The wind

stiffens his shoulders as the planter turns
back to the wicker gate, threshold, the hearth
and flame, the thought of a mulled aperitif,
the violin waiting by the lampstand,
and then his threadbare mourning shawl

already warmed by Sally's serving hands.

Monticello

Every story begins here. A father's face
Minted again and again until what you have
Is a nation. People keep saying
Slavery's complicated, but I don't believe them.
At night I wander the land. The orchard
Is our father's. Even you—standing,
Commanding, born emancipated—I see you
Traipsing the rows some nights, too, and
When the wind makes that hollow, leaden,
Begging sound, you falter. Brother,
Do you ever wonder what created our father?
I believe it is stealthy, leonine, a beast mad
To devour its own young. The boughs are heavy,
Slung with fruit upon fruit, untouched. It drops,
Rots. But first it pleads with the ground.

Prairie Rotunda

The Monticello ladies politely call him, still,
    "Mister Jefferson," spokesman for sanity.
        And on north Texas plains, more arid
    than his "little mountain" landscape, we too have
something of his legacy, in stone and Kansas brick.

Our founders decreed a Georgian edifice, that their
    newborn school might retain timeless dominion
        over sprawling fields of Johnson grass.
    They named it Dallas Hall. They made it Texas-sized.
Jefferson's "academical village," arranged

"around an open square of grass and trees," here became
    a microcosm turning inward: classrooms,
        piano rooms, post office, chapel,
    laboratories, hamburger grill, barber shop:
all beneath a Palladian dome with stained-glass top.

The Pantheon? More like University-as-Mall.
    Jefferson lauded "the authority of
        nature and power of reason": the
    heart of his college was a fine library,
not a church. Robert Frost and Carl Sandburg visited

our place in the 1920s. A decade before,
    SMU's president mounted a small hill,
        said, "This is where Dallas Hall will stand."
    His wife looked out at nothing, a shack and a
sad, deserted mule barn. She sighed, "You have lost your mind.

"You can't build a university in the middle
    of the prairie." Mister Jefferson would have

understood. Authority, nature,
power, and reason—Enlightenment values—
here turned columnar in the pursuit of happiness.

Sight Lines

I'm walking in sight of the Río Nambe—

salt cedar rises through silt in an irrigation ditch—

the snowpack in the Sangre de Cristos has already dwindled before
spring—

at least no fires erupt in the conifers above Los Alamos—

the plutonium waste has been hauled to an underground site—

a man who built plutonium triggers breeds horses now—

no one could anticipate this distance from Monticello—

Jefferson despised newspapers, but no one thing takes us out of
ourselves—

during the Cultural Revolution, a boy saw his mother shot in front
of a firing squad—

a woman detonates when a spam text triggers bombs strapped to
her body—

when I come to an upright circular steel lid, I step out of the
ditch—

I step out of the ditch but step deeper into myself—

I arrive at a space that no longer needs autumn or spring—

I find ginseng where there is no ginseng my talisman of desire—

though you are visiting Paris, you are here at my fingertips—

though I step back into the ditch, no whitening cloud dispels this
world's mystery—

the ditch ran before the year of the Louisiana Purchase—

I'm walking on silt, glimpsing horses in the field—

fielding the shapes of our bodies in white sand—

though parallel lines touch in the infinite, the infinite is here—

Pursuit

Plants are from a sly dimension.
With beguiling heads,
they run for the light,
their loves and their hates
undetected. They run and they run,
and never leave bed.
Even the great white oak,
with birds in the nest,
is in bed on Monticello,
where the grapes are asleep
in rows, drinking the sun,
turning the truth into serum.
And when Happiness comes for a sip,
she pays with her smile and hair,
then gives up her legs for a cup,
and then her right mind,
which is making its bed in the bottle.
How could that man not know,
the one who loves liberty and flowers,
that Happiness runs parallel to truth,
and can't have property,
and cannot cross it.

Graveyard, Monticello

Light silts through tulip poplars, waving.

Light gilds granite stones. Winds
hold renegade voices, fugitive

of the ravenous grave.
Roving, grieving, a confederate cry:

Hey hullah nonny fiddle honey-child o—
"My two hands grubbed." Jefferson's hands: his slaves.

Coffins built
in the Susquehanna foothills of the *forever mountains.*

Appalatio Mountains. An old west their horizon.
Now in the graveyard of these colonials,

unfinished lamentation:
Little stone, baby stone. Granite cracked with lichen.

Portal to the gone world, the old world. *Hush now.*
All your daddy's rages and drink can grow silent,

like a cruel overseer sent at last away.

Double Sonnet for Monticello's Grounds

if the weather is neither soft nor open
    when the first daughter learns to crawl
the father sends a box of thorns to the cellar

    if the deepest snow he's seen on the mountain
covers another daughter and an infant son
    in march he sows a patch of latter peas

if a further daughter lives the great poplar rots
    from the inside and he takes its shade
to wash it in the pond and another daughter dies

    if this morning early frost is sufficient to kill
and the blue ridge white
    his wife falls ill and the last daughter after

when thaw first disturbs the red dirt
    he'll plant them in his nursery of thorns
    . . .
if at last the whole of his hedges
    encloses the two orchards the girl walks
her daughter inside her and feeds her green

    if the monthly strawberries arrive
in an earthen box her daughter dies
    and she bears another to red apples after

if in june the clover is mown and pitch pine
    in rows lines the new road to the river
her daughter lives her daughter dies her daughter lives

if weather nests its immensity in the vineyard
she brings two young boys up
    from the cellar in the box of thorns

and outlives the father into given time
    when the mill floods and the almonds follow flower

Enlightenment

In the portrait of Jefferson that hangs
    at Monticello, he is rendered two-toned:
his forehead white with illumination—

a lit bulb—the rest of his face in shadow,
    darkened as if the artist meant to contrast
his bright knowledge, its dark subtext.

By 1805, when Jefferson sat for the portrait,
    he was already linked to an affair
with his slave. Against a backdrop, blue

and ethereal, a wash of paint that seems
    to hold him in relief, Jefferson gazes out
across the centuries, his lips fixed as if

he's just uttered some final word.
    The first time I saw the painting, I listened
as my father explained the contradictions:

how Jefferson hated slavery, though—*out
    of necessity,* my father said—had to own
slaves; that his moral philosophy meant

he could not have fathered those children:
    would have been impossible, my father said.
For years we debated the distance between

word and deed. I'd follow my father from book
    to book, gathering citations, listen
as he named—like a field guide to Virginia—

each flower and tree and bird as if to prove
    a man's pursuit of knowledge is greater
than his shortcomings, the limits of his vision.

I did not know then the subtext
    of our story, that my father could imagine
Jefferson's words made flesh in my flesh—

the improvement of the blacks in body
    and mind, in the first instance of their mixture
with the whites—or that my father could believe

he'd made me *better.* When I think of this now,
    I see how the past holds us captive,
its beautiful ruin etched on the mind's eye:

my young father, a rough outline of the old man
    he's become, needing to show me
the better measure of his heart, an equation

writ large at Monticello. That was years ago.
    Now, we take in how much has changed:
talk of Sally Hemings, someone asking,

How white was she?—parsing the fractions
    as if to name what made her worthy
of Jefferson's attentions: a near-white,

quadroon mistress, not a plain black slave.
    Imagine stepping back into the past,
our guide tells us then—and I can't resist

whispering to my father: *This is where*
    we split up. I'll head around to the back.
When he laughs, I know he's grateful

I've made a joke of it, this history
    that links us—white father, black daughter—
even as it renders us other to each other.

Jefferson Composing His Bible

> I composed the operation for my own use by cutting verse by verse out
> of the printed book and arranging the matter which is evidently his.

Candlelight, straight razor, ruler, an umber King James.
    Nearly midnight: unwigged, in his nightshirt,
        He's set his pantograph away & the house

Slave Ursula has brought him port, a bit of stilton.
    Jefferson is raising Lazarus, four days entombed—
        O take away *take away the stone.* Mary redacted,

Who goeth to the grave to weep there. Redacted too
    The one that was dead, the one bound head & foot
        With gravecloth, his face bound about with a napkin.

The one who in Giotto stands flanked
    With a crowd who mask their faces—not to hide their awe
        But to endure his stench. The one who

Caravaggio props naked in the arms of thugs,
    Rigor-mortised to cruciform, but goldening as
        The wonder-working arm reaches out. *Lazarus come forth.*

& Jefferson's razor commences its business. Along the ruler
    The slicing begins: John 11 entire. The gash extended,
        Acute & violent as Open Heart, though when he cuts

His index finger, three drops of blood—it must be the port!—
    Ensanguine the chief priest & Pharisees
        As they plot in the temple to take Him away.

& the operation is complete. He sets his hexagon
    Of superstition down, one more blow for reason,
        For the reason that shall free us from

The mere abracadabra of the mountebanks
    Calling themselves the priests of Jesus. Marginal,
        Illiterate, a barefoot rabbi who spoke some truths.

June at Monticello, the window by his desk stands open.
    Sussurant click of cricket & peeper, a slather of fireflies
        Darting the okra & broad beans of the kitchen garden.

Candle flicker. The night wind gently turns
    The Good Book's pages, its vellum windows shorn of miracle.
        The words remaining—*sublime, benevolent, & easily
        distinguishable*

As diamonds on a dunghill. O boundless are the mysteries
    Of the visible world. Pantograph, the quill pen
        Tempered, the rubied port & its quickening thrall.

The razor on his desk sits locked.

    for the Rev. Alane Cameron Miles

Christmas East of the Blue Ridge

So autumn comes to an end with these few wet sad stains
Stuck to the landscape,
                                December dark
Running its hands through the lank hair of late afternoon,
Little tongues of the rain holding forth
                                                under the eaves,
Such wash, such watery words . . .

So autumn comes to this end,
And winter's vocabulary, downsized and distanced,
Drop by drop
Captures the conversation with its monosyllabic gutturals
And tin music,
                    gravelly consonants, scratched vowels.

Soon the camel drivers will light their fires, soon the stars
Will start on their brief dip down from the back of heaven,
Down to the desert's dispensation
And night reaches, the gall and first birth,
The second only one word from now,
                                one word and its death from right now.

Meanwhile, in Charlottesville, the half-moon
Hums like a Hottentot
                            high over Monticello,
Clouds dishevel and rag out,
The alphabet of our discontent
Keeps on with its lettering,
                            gold on the black walls of our hearts . . .

On Imagination

from Homage to Phillis Wheatley

> Religion indeed has produced a Phyllis Wheatley; but it could not
> produce a poet.
> —Thomas Jefferson, *Notes on the State of Virginia*

First poet of your Race,
you could be nothing but servant
in these States—learning R's
to say *The Lord,* not learning *you*
but *Thou.* How thy face

lit up among the oil lamps each week
you had to clean! Sable
sister—at least your master
did not make you with him
(we think) sleep, or

out in the stable. Your world was now
whispers and *Sincerely's*—on the block
Master Wheatley bought you off,
you must have thought (though most thought
you could not):—Such strange beasts

haggling over me! My head must
stay covered, my must must
not show. I shall be the girl's
plaything, taking orders, learning
to write in order to tell them

what I am not. Thankful,
yes, I am for that:—for the Ink
which ran darker even than I

and which I could flood the world
with; for Temperance; for Faith

which lets me know what I must do,—
bend, bow my head and knee.
Be humble, so saieth Thee
and they, my family, who does not know
my *first* name. My quill feather flies

across the page. I wait.

I first came to live in Charlottesville, Virginia, just across the Rivanna River from Thomas Jefferson's birthplace in Shadwell, in 1974. That was the year I entered the University of Virginia as a member of one of the first mixed-gender classes admitted to what is still known to many as "Mr. Jefferson's University." I went on to earn a graduate degree there, and after seven years spent teaching at universities in other towns, in 1989 I returned to Charlottesville. Since then I have raised a family here and taught in the University's Department of English for over twenty years. Thanks largely to my three children and to my life here as a student and then professor, I have visited Monticello countless times—on my own, on school field trips, and in the company of visitors to the University. Monticello, the house Jefferson built and rebuilt for most of his life, sits on a little mountain overlooking the town, and is now protected by a foundation committed to historical preservation, excavation, reparation, and education. Over four hundred thousand tourists, scholars, and others visit the site each year.

It is impossible to overstate the ways in which Jefferson saturates both his "academical village" and its environs. Jefferson has unknowingly lent his name to gravestone makers and insurance companies, dentist offices and midwifery groups, sandwiches and cocktails. An object of intense projection, Jefferson is treated alike with blind adoration (it's not unusual, especially on Founder's Day, to see an actor dressed as Jefferson walking the Grounds, shaking hands and taking selfies with students) and with bemused irony (while in residence at the University, artist Michael Krueger did a series of prints depicting a drunken Jefferson wandering amid the ubiquitous red Solo cups in front of a UVA frat house). A signboard for the University's copy shop shows Jefferson in a pair of Ray Bans.

But polarized and oversimplified responses to Jefferson and his paradoxes are not just local to Charlottesville. Based on documentary and scientific evidence, most historians now believe that Jefferson, after the death of his wife, conceived six children with his slave Sally Hemings, adding fuel to the ongoing racial tension that is pandemic in twenty-first-century America. Jefferson's struggles in his own time abide with regard to the limits and reach of the federal government (and the country's citizens) in matters of economics, war, gender, and religious and personal freedom. That many tensions faced by the nation at its founding are unrelieved in national life contributes to opinions about Jefferson that can be as murky and myriad as the issues themselves.

Just this past fall, on a visit to Monticello with the poet Brian Teare, I heard another visitor, when asked by a tour guide why Thomas Jefferson might have chosen not to free his slaves even when he claimed to despise the institution of slavery, respond, "Isn't it because the freed slaves couldn't have survived on their own in the world without Jefferson's protection?" I was relieved when our tour guide quickly responded: "No, that's not it. Jefferson couldn't *afford* to let his slaves go. He needed them to do the work required to build this house and maintain his lifestyle, something he did not have the cash flow to do." As Ravi Shankar asks in "Thomas Jefferson in Kathmandu," "Democracy is a fine ideal yet to be supplanted, / but does it coexist with capitalism?" Clearly there's still a long way to go in understanding and interpreting our nation's contradictory matrix, with its promise of liberty, justice, and equality for all.

As *Salon* put it in 2012: "Every spin on the third president appears at first to have merit. Jefferson has been a political symbol since he first sought the presidency, and a piñata in America's culture wars for nearly as long as that." This anthology, however, has no set political or cultural agenda. It is a poetic project, not a scholarly or historical one. Luckily, anyone interested in learning about the historical Jefferson can do so thanks to a seemingly unending flood of often contradictory scholarly studies, popular books, biographies, and edited primary sources. Perhaps most notable among recent books are Jon Meacham's *Thomas Jefferson: The Art of Power* (2012) and Annette Gordon-Reed's *The Hemingses of Monticello: An Ameri-*

can Family (2008). Ongoing research and outreach education by the Thomas Jefferson Foundation at Monticello provide other sources of continually updated information, serving, too, as a clearinghouse for other historical sites, archives, and resources.

It is my hope that this anthology of twentieth- and twenty-first-century poems about Thomas Jefferson makes a fresh, unique contribution to what must be an ongoing conversation for Americans.

Debra Allbery (1957) is the author most recently of *Fimbul-Winter.* Her awards include two fellowships from the National Endowment for the Arts, a Hawthornden fellowship, and two grants from the New Hampshire State Council on the Arts. She has taught in the MFA Program for Writers at Warren Wilson College since 1995 and has served as the program's director since 2009.

"An Ordinary Portion of Life": Jefferson was a prolific writer of letters, an epistolary habit that did not abate with age. After a long rift with his former ally and then nemesis John Adams, and at the instigation of Benjamin Rush, Jefferson renewed his correspondence with Adams, and in their later years missives passed back and forth regularly between the two Founding Fathers. Debra Allbery calls "An Ordinary Portion of Life" essentially a found poem. In it, she makes use of Jefferson's practice of citing in his late letters passages from the then immensely popular poem "Night Thoughts" by Edward Young, a poet Jefferson revered and whose work he often copied into the Commonplace Book he kept in his twenties. An epistolary poem spoken in Jefferson's voice, "An Ordinary Portion of Life" weaves Jefferson's words, under the spell of Allbery's own imaginings, with remembered passages from Young's "The Third Night," which laments a repetitive life. Allbery conjures Jefferson in old age, as he takes stock of his limitations and achievements and looks with restive curiosity to the future. The moving last stanza is Jefferson, verbatim.

Talvikki Ansel (1962) is the author of *My Shining Archipelago* (Yale Series of Younger Poets Award), *Jetty & other poems,* and *Somewhere In Space* (Ohio University Press/*The Journal* Award in Poetry). She worked in the gardens at Monticello in the late 1980s, and her haphazard garden in Rhode Island has a few familiar varieties from

Jefferson's estate: blackberry lily, "tennis ball" lettuce, and a tulip poplar.

From "Works and Days": Talvikki Ansel helped to tend the gardens of Monticello for two years between taking her undergraduate and graduate degrees. These passages are excerpted from a longer poem that includes, in addition to a series of nine-line stanzas, marginal notations, telegraphic jottings from a notebook, and reminders to the speaker about certain horticultural tasks, seeds, plant development, and so forth. This series, which follows the trajectory of the seasons and alludes to Hesiod in its title, is full of the names of things—places, plants, birds, trees—and in this respect reflects Jefferson's own obsessive cataloguing and listing of the flora and fauna at Monticello. In the third section, Ansel mentions that "two tulip / poplars frame the house"; recent visitors to Monticello know that one of those trees, standing when Jefferson was alive, was diseased and had to be cut down, though the massive trunk with its annular rings remains, a reminder, like Ansel's poem, of the palimpsestic layering of the place.

Gabrielle Calvocoressi (1974) is the author of *The Last Time I Saw Amelia Earhart* and *Apocalyptic Swing,* which was a finalist for the Los Angeles Times Books Prize. She has been the recipient of numerous awards and fellowships, among them a Stegner Fellowship and Jones Lectureship from Stanford University and a Rona Jaffe Woman Writer's Award. She is Senior Poetry Editor at *Los Angeles Review of Books* and teaches at the University of North Carolina at Chapel Hill.

"Monticello Smokehouse Festivity": Working in an invented form she calls a "festivity," Gabrielle Calvocoressi creates in "Monticello Smokehouse Festivity" a kind of choral work, full of incremental repetition, that allows her to give the poem many speakers. One can imagine a host of singers calling up this house into being—family members (legitimate and illegitimate), enslaved people, indentured servants, overseers, visitors. As the poem gathers momentum, its darknesses deepen ("Belly / heaving on the ground and bruised where you fell"), reminding us that all great houses belonging to complex histories are replete with secrets and transgressions. Particularly powerful is the way Calvocoressi's choice of a plural speaker avoids, finally, blaming any one culprit; all of the voices are complicit in their awarenesses, and even though the "festivity" is meant to be "sung at high volume, by a large group, in rounds, so the house shakes," the silence surrounding that boisterous clamor is stridently present and eloquent as well. House converges with body, speaker with reader, in ways that illuminate and disturb in equal measure.

John Casteen (1971) is the author of two books of poems, *Free Union* and *For the Mountain Laurel.* His poems and essays have appeared in *Virginia Quarterly Review,* the *Paris Review, Fence,* the *Morning News,* and *Best American Poetry.* He lives in Earlysville, Virginia.

"The Jefferson Bible": In 1820, while in his seventies, Thomas Jefferson undertook the production of what he would call *The Life and Morals of Jesus of Nazareth,* a redaction of the four Biblical Gospels intended to bring them into line with his own sense of what was and wasn't trustworthy in those texts. With a sharp instrument, Jefferson excised from six copies of the New Testament (in Latin, French, Greek, and King James English) those passages that he felt truly reflected the teachings of Christ. He then pasted these excerpts onto blank papers in four columns, English and French on one side, Latin and Greek on the facing pages. He later had the volume bound into what is now known as the Jefferson Bible (and for many years, until the 1950s when the first facsimile run ran out, every newly elected United States senator received a copy of said Bible when he or she took the oath of office). Casteen's poem braids politics, poetry, belief, and the museum of history to "hold open" a way to approach our human contradictions: with compassion, with query.

Jennifer Chang (1976) is the author of *The History of Anonymity*. Her poems have appeared in the *Nation,* the *New Republic, Poetry,* and *A Public Space,* and she has published essays on poetry in the *Los Angeles Review of Books, Blackwell's Companion to the Harlem Renaissance,* and the *Volta.* She is Assistant Professor of English and Creative Writing at the George Washington University and lives in Washington, D.C.

"A Horse Named Never": Jefferson loved horses since boyhood, and long before he began to build Monticello he roamed the mountain's environs on horseback. After his wife died, he spent weeks in a kind of fugue state, wandering the pitches and slopes astride a horse, often accompanied by his eldest daughter. He was even able to ride in advanced age—nearing 80, he still rode, by his own account, "without fatigue 6. or 8. miles every day and sometimes 20." As an adult, he kept several horses in stables close to the house, but others were quartered elsewhere on the mountain and cared for by an array of enslaved and hired people. In Jennifer Chang's poem, the speaker—a slave, perhaps an illegitimate son—dwells in Jefferson's realm; but, like the horses and the bastard son Chang evokes in her paraphrase of a comment from William Butler Yeats about *King Lear,* the narrator can "neither flee nor be kept." Witness to "the gardens overlooking this deplorable entanglement, our country," the speaker is the wise "fool that has faith in Never," with all that such uneasy trust implies both for and against change and possibility.

Lucille Clifton (1936–2010) was the author of fourteen books of poetry as well as many award-winning children's books. Her many honors include a National Endowment for the Arts Fellowship, the National Book Award, and the Ruth Lilly Prize given to a living U.S. poet to honor extraordinary achievement. She served as Poet Laureate of Maryland and was honored with the Poetry Society of America's Robert Frost Medal for Lifetime Achievement after her death.

"monticello": Never one to shy away from complexity, Lucille Clifton is a poet well known for her wit, economy of language, and appreciation of the emotional stamina of survivors. No surprise, then, that she takes on the mythical declarer of independence in order to call him out on the passel of red-haired children among the enslaved population of Monticello. Characteristically lean and epigrammatic, Clifton's "monticello" evokes contemporary satirical poems that addressed rumors about Jefferson and Sally Hemings, such as this 1806 verse from a longer poem by Irish poet Thomas Moore:

> The weary statesman for repose has fled
> From halls of council to his negro's shed,
> Where blest he woos some black Aspasia's grace,
> And dreams of freedom in his slave's embrace!

In Clifton's brief lyric, God trumps Jefferson (and perhaps stands in for him—as Jefferson said, he felt a "sect" unto himself), declaring "no independence." But what follows is a saucy, insistent evocation of the body's truth and survival. With what poet Kazim Ali calls the dactylic "rhythmic levity" of the last line, Clifton chooses to privilege not the oppressor but the bold, bright endurance of the branded.

Michael Collier (1953) is the author of six books of poetry including *The Ledge,* which was a finalist for the National Book Critics Circle Award and the *Los Angeles Times* Book Prize. He has published a collection of essays about poetry and the writing life titled *Make Us Wave Back,* edited three poetry anthologies, and produced a translation of Euripides's *Medea.* A former Maryland State Poet Laureate, he teaches at the University of Maryland and is the Director of the Bread Loaf Writers' Conference.

"Jefferson's Bees": Jefferson was curious about bees, as he was about almost everything. Poets, both ancient and modern, have also seemed to find bees—their behavior, hierarchies, instincts, and rituals—fascinating. In "Jefferson's Bees," Michael Collier weaves personal history—such as his exposure to his mother's casual, unthinking racism ("she who called / Brazil nuts, *nigger toes*")—with details from Jefferson's notes and books. The resulting poem shows the unsettling parallels between the work of the hive and the workings of a Virginia plantation ("these exotics known by natives as the white man's flies"), culminating in the present time, in which the hives are, "like everything / at Monticello, restored to an idea, one that's survived its own foreclosure."

Stephen Cushman (1956) has published ten books of poetry and scholarship, most recently *The Red List: A Poem* and *Belligerent Muse: Five Northern Writers and How They Shaped Our Understanding of the Civil War.* He is Robert C. Taylor Professor of English at the University of Virginia, where he has taught for more than thirty years and been named Cavaliers' Distinguished Teaching Professor for 2014–16.

"Cut and Paste": Like John Casteen, Ron Slate, and David Wojahn, Stephen Cushman responds, in his own way, to Jefferson's Bible, his "roll-your-own gospel." What Jefferson tended to leave out, as Cushman's poem tells us, is anything that seemed "unreasonable," anything with a hint of the miraculous—the turning of water into wine, the raising of the dead, making the blind man see. However, as Cushman warns, "cutting and pasting / may deepen blindness, taste self-perpetuating handcuff itself, / got to paste in some challenges too." Cushman presses in, suggesting that any real appreciation for religious freedom must include not only religious expressions from the Western world but those of indigenous, often exploited peoples as well: "let's push the statute, let's worship freely, / Jaya Ganesha or the Tryambakam, . . . / . . . or worship like a Miwok climbing up through / the tonsure of tree line in springtime Yosemite." Cushman's last lines suggest the perils of any redacted history: "it's up to you, you get to choose / whether to include, whether omit, Yosemite meant killers."

Kate Daniels (1953) is the author of four books of poetry, most recently *A Walk in Victoria's Secret,* and editor of two volumes, including Muriel Rukeyser's selected poems, *Out of Silence.* She is a former Guggenheim Fellow in Poetry and a member of the Fellowship of Southern Writers. Currently, she is Professor of English and Director of Creative Writing at Vanderbilt University.

"Reading a Biography of Thomas Jefferson in the Months of My Son's Recovery": As the title of her poem signals, Kate Daniels revisits Thomas Jefferson in light of the difficult hospitalization and recovery of a troubled son, who suffers from bipolar disorder, a familial affliction that "stalk[s] him / Threatening his freedom / And his right to self-rule." Of Jefferson, Daniels writes, "Can't help drawing back at how he lived in two minds / Because he was *of two minds* like a person / With old time manic depression: the slaveholder / And the Democrat, the tranquil hilltop of Monticello, / And the ringing cobblestones of Paris, France." The struggles of the young man and of Jefferson are juxtaposed in provocative ways: "The way two things can coexist without / Cancelling each other out—how did he live / Like that? *How does my son live like that?*" Finally, Daniels writes, "His language stirs me up." As poet, mother, and citizen, she seeks "in the painful / Contradictions of his personal life and public / Service, ongoing signs for how to live / In *this* strange era."

Rita Dove (1952) is the author of nine poetry collections, most recently *Sonata Mulattica.* In 2011 she edited *The Penguin Anthology of Twentieth-Century American Poetry.* A former U.S. Poet Laureate (1993–95) and recipient of the 1987 Pulitzer Prize for *Thomas and Beulah,* she has also published fiction, drama, and essays. Among her numerous honors are the 1996 National Humanities Medal and the 2011 National Medal of Arts. She is Commonwealth Professor of English at the University of Virginia.

"What Doesn't Happen": "What Doesn't Happen" comes from Rita Dove's book-length sequence *Sonata Mulattica,* which tells the story of the eighteenth-century child prodigy George Augustus Polgreen Bridgetower, son of an Afro-Caribbean father and a Polish-German mother. Blending historical fact and poetic imaginings, Dove explores the ironies and exhilarations of this biracial violin virtuoso, who knew Hayden and inspired Beethoven, and whom Thomas Jefferson saw perform in Paris in 1789. "What Doesn't Happen" recounts the nine-year-old Bridgetower's carriage ride to the Salles des Machines and subsequent performance there. In a brilliant stroke of poetic license, she imagines Bridgetower noticing not only Jefferson in the audience but, more importantly, a girl beside him who is "dark, dark yet warm / as the violin's nut-brown sheen . . ." While serving Jefferson and his daughters during their Parisian stay, Sally Hemings was paid wages; she, along with her brother James, could have stayed in Paris as a free person instead of returning with the family to Virginia as a slave. That this didn't happen not only shaped the course of Hemings's, Jefferson's, and their children's lives but embodies the profound and disturbing nexus of power and submission that characterizes slavery.

Claudia Emerson (1957–2014) was the author of six collections of poetry, including *The Opposite House: Poems,* published posthumously in 2015. She was winner of the Pulitzer Prize in 2006 and Poet Laureate of Virginia from 2008–10. A gifted teacher, she taught at the University of Mary Washington for many years. In 2013 she joined the creative writing faculty at Virginia Commonwealth University, where she taught until her untimely death from colon cancer in December 2014.

"Ungrafted: Jefferson's Vines": Jefferson is well known to have loved wine, to have consumed it daily in moderation, and to have made several attempts to grow it on the terraces of his mountain home. Claudia Emerson's sonnet begins from Jefferson's failure to consider grafting European root stock with the stock of "blander" but hardier native grapes, a procedure vital to wine growing today. But by the middle of the octave, we realize that Emerson is talking about more than viticulture. On one hand, she's speaking of the new nation, and to the anxiety of Jefferson and the other founders' great experiment: can we sever from European stock completely or are we better off grafting our native stock with the old? On the other hand, issues of nature versus control, restriction versus freedom, also speak to matters in Jefferson's personal life. "What you might have made the candle-flame entered anyway," she writes, "the red quickening, evening a slip like a blade / into it." That "quickening" is certainly meant to suggest Jefferson's other "graftings"—the mixing of his own blood with that of Sally Hemings: "that was the graft / of what you did with what you might have done— / what might have become the tongue, becoming it."

Nick Flynn (1960), is a poet, playwright, and essayist. Since 2004 he has been a professor on the creative writing faculty at the University of Houston, where he is in residence each spring. His most recent book is *My Feelings,* a collection of poems. His work has been translated into fifteen languages.

"When I Was a Girl": In "When I Was a Girl," Nick Flynn explores the ways in which children, instinctively and through education, play-enact scenarios of power, hierarchy, enslavement, usurpation, and submission that belong to the world they inhabit but only partially comprehend. As the children take turns swapping roles as boy and girl, master and slave, the poem dilates into an almost pre-Lapsarian landscape in which "girls ran across burning fields // with swords made of sticks, girls / hid in trees, stones heavy in their / hands." The last, powerful image of the poem, in which we see how freedom might turn into violence ("If a bird landed in my palm // I could either crush it / or set it free"), refers to a private letter of 1803 from Jefferson to William Henry Harrison, in which Jefferson, speaking of Native Americans, writes, "As to their fear, we presume that our strength and their weakness is now so visible that they must see we have only to shut our hand to crush them, and that all our liberalities to them proceed from motives of pure humanity only."

Gabriel Fried (1974), is the author of a poetry collection, *Making the New Lamb Take,* and editor of *Heart of the Order: Baseball Poems.* He is the longtime director of the American poetry series at Persea Books.

"Letter from Poplar Forest": Poplar Forest is a retreat Jefferson built for himself between 1806 and 1809 in Bedford County, Virginia, about a day's ride from Monticello. Jefferson often repaired there, sometimes with family members, when he had business in that part of Virginia or when he wanted to escape the hectic world of Monticello. In August 1815, Jefferson wrote from Poplar Forest to his granddaughter Martha Randolph, who was at Monticello, that the peaches at Poplar Forest were as abundant and sweet as those in Albemarle County. Gabriel Fried uses this letter to trigger a memory of the speaker's own "northeast orchards," with their peaches so exotic as to be "pheromonal." When Martha received Jefferson's letter, on the cusp of thirteen, she could not have known that shortly after her heavily indebted grandfather died, her family would be forced to sell Monticello and, eventually, Poplar Forest, including the paradisiacal orchards. But the poem allows us to venture into that future: "as if a young girl, in the thrall / of such sweet-smelling legacy, might know / what one day she will fling aside—which / pits—and what she will cling to."

Carmen Gillespie (1965) is Director of the Griot Institute at Bucknell University, where she teaches literature and creative writing. In addition to literary criticism, Gillespie has published a poetry chapbook, *Lining the Rails,* and a full-length collection, *Jonestown: A Vexation,* which won the Naomi Long Madgett Poetry Prize. She has been the recipient of grants from the National Endowment for the Humanities, the Mellon Foundation, and the Bread Loaf Writer's Conference.

"Monticello Duet: Outside/In": In her dramatic, script-like poem, Carmen Gillespie intersperses passages from the dictated memoir of Isaac Jefferson, a former Monticello slave also known as

Isaac Granger after he was freed, with imagined voicings from the viewpoint of Sally Hemings. Isaac was the son of two very important Monticello slaves—Great George, who eventually became the overseer, and Ursula, a much valued and trusted house slave. In 1847, when he was 72, he provided a short oral account of his life at Monticello. Isaac was an "outside" slave, working as a tinsmith and blacksmith, while Sally worked primarily inside the house, but Gillespie presses in to show us more than just the distinct experiences of two different kinds of slave. Isaac's "public" testimony contrasts powerfully with Gillespie's lyric intuition of Sally Hemings's thoughts, his matter-of-fact talk about mountain fires, lightning strikes, clocks, and gates illuminating her interior musings on Eros, sorrow, and language. Gillespie gives Sally the last sound, if not word; the poem ends with her "ummm hmmm," part consent, part prayer response, part sound of a gate opening.

Aracelis Girmay (1977) is the author of the poetry collections *Teeth* (GLCA New Writers Award) and *Kingdom Animalia* (Isabella Gardner Award; finalist for the National Book Critics Circle Award). She is the author/collagist of *changing, changing*. Her newest project, which looks at immigration, the refugee crisis, and crossings by Eritreans over the Mediterranean Sea, is slated for publication in 2016. Girmay teaches in the School for Interdisciplinary Arts at Hampshire College.

"[*american verses,* excerpt]": The title and last line of Aracelis Girmay's poem evoke and converse with Robert Hayden's "[American Journal]," in which an alien narrator visits America in an attempt to understand the place. Girmay starts her foray with an excavation of "the Jeffersonian dry well / in Monticello's yard" and then "braid[s]" the poem, like the speaker's hair, in "three directions": personal, historical, and imaginative. As a woman of color growing up in America, the speaker conceives of herself as "half statement, half question": "./? I am, / in the long, dark throat of the republic, / standing now, the inconceivable result / of the experiment." The poem asks, among other things: how does personal history, particularly the history of the body, engage with other histories and with the body that is language? In its hybrid plurality, this rich poem explores the "[b]lood" and "[h]istory of conjunctions," a protean admixture upon which notions of individuality and community depend.

Paul Guest (1974) is the author of four full-length collections of poetry and a memoir, *One More Theory about Happiness*. His awards include a Guggenheim Fellowship and a Whiting Award. He teaches at the University of Virginia.

"Monticello": Perhaps because a nickel won't buy much anymore, most Americans likely pay little attention to the minted images of Jefferson and his house when they're dropping spare change into the tip jar at Starbucks. The speaker in Paul Guest's poem acknowledges that he himself gave Monticello and Jefferson little thought except when his grandfather used to quiz him about historical trivia in exchange for pocket money. What happens when what we feel in response to an iconic place disappoints or disturbs or disillusions us in some way? Guest's speaker describes his one brief visit to Monticello, cut short by his fear that his wheelchair might cause damage as he wends through the glass doors and cordoned-off rooms. On his drive back down the mountain, the speaker conflates his complicated feelings about the house visit with regret at not being able to attend his grandfather's funeral the previous year: "I left and it was dark / outside and below us / glowing ribbons wound into town. / That night, the stars, / this poem like apology." The poem confronts the entangled feelings of guilt and regret that often accompany the convergence of personal and historical stories.

Robert Hass (1941) is the author of *The Apple Trees at Olema: Selected Poems* and *What Light Can Do: Selected Essays*. He is Professor of English at the University of California at Berkeley. His many awards include the Pulitzer Prize, the National Book Award, and the National Book Critics Circle Award. He served as United States Poet Laureate from 1995–97.

"Monticello": For all its spare elegance and anachronistic wit, Robert Hass's "Monticello" has, like the best political poems, a core of ardent, eloquent ire. After some playful imagining (Jefferson trawling the aisles of the Charlottesville K-Mart, for instance), the poem darkens: "I try to think of history: the mammoth / jawbone in the entry hall, / Napoleon in marble, / Meriwether Lewis dead at Grinder's Trace." These relics of dominion and the detail about Lewis's possible suicide lead the speaker even deeper into his argument for equality and transparency: "I don't want the powers separated, / . . . / private places / in the public weal / that ache against the teeth like ice." Although the poem ends with one of the loveliest images in contemporary poetry, the reader registers that "star-shaped" fall of snow in the mouth (ice against the teeth) as well as in the "vaginal leaves of old magnolias," a reminder that any real sense of history must belong to the vicissitudes and passions of the living world, to living memory, and to the living voice.

Terrance Hayes (1971) is the author of *Lighthead,* winner of the 2010 National Book Award. His other books are *Wind in a Box, Hip Logic, Muscular Music,* and, most recently, *How to Be Drawn.* His honors include a National Endowment for the Arts Fellowship, a Guggenheim Fellowship, and a 2014 MacArthur Fellowship.

"A Poem Inspired by a Frederick Douglass Middle Schooler's Essay on Thomas Jefferson": Terrance Hayes's poem lets the reader know, from the get-go enjambment of the title into the first line, to expect a dizzying, metatextual slippage of expectation and subversion, of footnotes and glosses, all in a stereoscopic mash-up of irony, wit, anger, and tenderness. While the poem announced in the title may not get written, what is written instead includes tangents and samplings that plunder racist passages from Jefferson's *Notes on the State of Virginia,* spiral out onto the pop-culturally savvy and edgy margins of Los Angeles, and move into the legacies of African Americans: their personhood, their art, their "being." Among the many gifts of this poem is its shout-out to the homeless artist "Red" ("who as you can see looks a lot like Thomas Jefferson!"), whose

YouTube video, named in the poem, would, or should, compel anyone to think anew about the "apocryphal third president" and the ongoing experiment that is America.

Brenda Hillman (1951) is the author of nine books of poetry, including a tetralogy on the elements; her most recent volume, *Seasonal Works With Letters on Fire,* won the Griffin International Prize for Poetry. She has also edited several volumes of poetry and prose, including *Poems from Under the Hill* by Libyan poet Ashur Etwebi and *Instances* by Korean poet Jeonrye Choi. She is the Olivia C. Filippi Professor of Poetry at Saint Mary's College of California.

"Near the Rim of the Ideal": Brenda Hillman's "Near the Rim of the Ideal" finds its speaker traveling home by air "from the east." As she grapples with her anger over recent horrors in Gaza and the Ukraine, "the concept of *nation* / stalls in the bitter brain," and a meditation on the "founding fathers" and on Jefferson in particular ("why / did he think he deserved all that?") ensues. The poem is strengthened by Hillman's refusal to demonize Jefferson completely—when she calls him a "paradox, finest of / men," she is not being ironic entirely, though she clearly wants no truck with any sort of "natural law" unless it is "the law of the rock & dirt not / my country 'tis of trading metals & cloth / carried on the backs of children." Appropriating the language of Jefferson's Declaration of Independence, Hillman digs deep down into "Jefferson's garden," refusing to hold as self-evident any truths of empire or nation "if specifics fail." The poem enacts its own diving into the wreck of national experience, suggesting that a nation is a matter of humanity. Its closing passage, ambiguous in its suggestion of nationless vulnerability to infection, is a call for a new way of seeing and being.

Mark Jarman (1952) is the author of over a dozen books of poetry and prose, most recently *Bone Fires: New and Selected Poems.* He is Centennial Professor of English at Vanderbilt University, where he has taught for over thirty years. Awards for his work include the

Lenore Marshall Prize from the Academy of American Poets and the Poets' Prize.

"Nora's Nickel": Mark Jarman's loose double sonnet appears, on first read, to be itself "a little story" about a ritual between a grand-mother and her grandson, a vignette about a lost nickel and the importance of making offerings, however small, on behalf of others less fortunate than ourselves. As the first fourteen-line stanza hinges into the second, however, we see that the Deep South where Grand-mother Nora grew up is a place of the past. She has herself been transplanted, not to China but to San Diego, and while she still car-ries with her some vestiges of her upbringing ("her okra simmering through the afternoon"), the grandson must resort to myth in order to understand the South. "The house she'd grown up in in Missis-sippi," Jarman writes, "I pictured as looking like the house on the nickel." Even at Monticello's most dilapidated, it is more likely that Nora's house resembled a servant's cabin than the mansion pictured on those saved-up coins, an irony lost on the boy at the time but communicated subtly and provocatively to the reader. Jarman also reminds us that the Red Indian and buffalo on Nora's older nickels represent another heavy price paid to pave "the way to San Diego."

Joan Naviyuk Kane (1977) is the author of *Hyperboreal* and *The Cormorant Hunter's Wife*. She has received a Whiting Award, the Donald Hall Prize in Poetry, an American Book Award, and fellow-ships from the Rasmuson Foundation and the School for Advanced Research. Inupiaq with family from King Island and Mary's Igloo, Alaska, she raises her children in Anchorage and teaches in the graduate writing program at the Institute of American Indian Arts in Santa Fe, New Mexico.

"Incognitum": Jefferson used his two-story entrance hall at Monti-cello as a kind of museum, calling it the "Indian Hall." Part of this room was devoted to a display of artifacts acquired from Native Americans by Lewis and Clark during their famous expedition to the west coast—the antlers and skins of various animals, as well as pottery, pipes, bows and arrows, and a painted buffalo robe. Jefferson had conflicting feelings about the indigenous peoples of the continent. He reminisced about boyhood encounters with Indians living in the Shadwell area, defended Native Americans in *Notes of the State of Virginia,* and wrote to the Marquis de Chastellux that he believed them "in body and mind equal to the whiteman." But when he perceived resistant tribes as impediments to the nation's development, he considered them "savages," and felt that his only recourse was to remove or crush them. Kane, an Inuit/Inupiaq poet, titles her poem after the American mammoth whose fossilized skeleton was discovered in 1801, and which Jefferson held up proudly as proof of the superior vitality of American fauna. Haunting Kane's poem is the specter of cultural extinction, a reprehensible byproduct of Manifest Destiny. That rich, myriad populations must now be "fallen together for excavation" in such a monument to America is both an ominous cry of "desolation" and a call for remediation.

Jennifer Key (1974) is the author of *The Old Dominion.* A former Diane Middlebrook Fellow at the University of Wisconsin, she has taught at the University of North Carolina at Pembroke and Southern Methodist University.

"Jefferson's Daughters": Jennifer Key's poem imagines what life must have been like for Jefferson's daughters when they returned as young women to Monticello after living in Paris. "Snowbound / in their father's great georgic experiment / while the social season whirls without them," the girls measure out their days in miles of embroidery thread, overseeing the larder and cellar (to which, at least, they hold the key) and "dust[ing] the jawbone of history / in the entrance hall." Key's poem reminds us that many in America, even among the moneyed classes, suffered from the fact of "freedom for a few and all that." The poem does not spare Jefferson's own implication in this set-up ("Oh, if there is a god here, // he enters the kitchen weekly / to wind the hands and let it go"). It will take the brave words and actions of many generations of Americans "for the age of reason / to finally see the light." That Key feminizes the established order in the last couplet is no accident: "The old dominion drowses half-asleep, / the fist of her buds less blossom than bomb."

Yusef Komunyakaa (1947) is the author of twenty-one books, most recently *The Emperor of Water Clocks.* He has been the recipient of numerous awards including the Pulitzer Prize, the Ruth Lilly Poetry Prize, the Poetry Society of America's Shelley Memorial Award, and the 2011 Wallace Stevens Award. His plays, performance art, and libretti have been performed internationally, and include *Wakonda's Dream, Saturnalia, Testimony,* and *Gilgamesh* (a verse play). He teaches at New York University.

"Daddy Hemmings Was Good with Curves": Yusef Komunyakaa's poem "Monticello," which appeared in *Taboo: Poems* (2004), is one of the poems that first inspired this anthology:

> Words: *I advance it,*
>
> *therefore, as a suspicion*
> *only, that the blacks . . .*
> *are inferior to the whites*
>
> *in the endowments of the body*
> *and mind.* As he talked & dined,
> did the women ever face
>
> each other like Philomela
> & Procne, a nightingale
> and swallow on some forked
>
> branch in their minds?

When I approached Komounyakaa about the possibility of reprinting this poem, he said that he'd welcome the chance to write a new poem about Jefferson and his world, a subject with which he "wasn't quite done." In this new poem, Komunyakaa focuses his illuminating lens on John Hemmings (1776–1833), half-brother of Sally Hemings. One of only five slaves freed in Jefferson's will, John (known as "Daddy" to Jefferson's grandchildren and others) was much trusted and beloved at Monticello, a gifted carpenter and "prime joiner," who not only crafted "sled, toy, cabinet, desk, / or Jefferson's landau carriage" but also is believed to have built Jefferson's coffin. Komunyakaa shows us that in "graft[ing] cherry // & mahogany, almost as one," "Daddy" was also grafting anew his own hybrid legacy, keeping aside a saving remnant of wood from one master's coffin to allow for the stitching, the repair, of his own agency and that of his descendants.

Maurice Manning (1966) has published five books, most recently *The Gone and the Going Away.* His first book was selected for the Yale Series of Younger Poets. His fourth book, *The Common Man,* was a finalist for the Pulitzer Prize. He teaches at Transylvania University in Lexington, Kentucky, and in the MFA Program for Writers at Warren Wilson College.

"Epiphanies": The word *epiphany* derives from the Greek *epiphaneia* and refers to a striking appearance or manifestation, often in com-memoration of the appearance of a god or other divinity. Christians use the word to refer to the appearance of Christ to the disciples and, in the liturgical calendar, to mark the visit to the Christ child by the three wise men. Manning may have these meanings in mind, but he is most likely evoking Thomas De Quincey's notion of a "flash of sublime revelation" experienced in the midst of "ordi-nary life," often in relation to a text. Manning considers Jefferson's rational temperament and Enlightenment tenets, and wonders if these ever allowed for the intrusion of the irrational or divine into a world whose beauty Jefferson certainly appreciated, catalogued, and attempted to control. Implicated in Manning's speculations about Jefferson across the vistas of the past are moral, political, and spiritual issues about which Jefferson and his generation, like ours, never reached a universal epiphany or mutual consensus. Interestingly, these musings create for Manning's speaker a kind of "mini-epiphany" that deepens his private understanding of Jefferson and Monticello.

Thorpe Moeckel (1971) is the author of six books of poetry and prose, most recently *Arcadia Road: A Trilogy.* He is Associate Professor at Hollins University, where he directs the Jackson Center for Creative Writing. His awards include a National Endowment for the Arts Fellowship, a Sustainable Arts Foundation Fellowship, and the George Garrett Award from the Fellowship of Southern Writers.

"On Hearing the Waterthrush Again, Jefferson": In this poem, Thorpe Moeckel conjures a day in Jefferson's life in March 1794. The day begins at dawn with an account of one of the protracted "fits of head-ache" that were to plague Jefferson for much of his life, but it also allows time for a walk, on which he hears a number of birds—"parula, cardinal, . . . / a blue winged teal . . . , // countless geese." It is hearing the waterthrush, however, with its evocation of wings and molt, "vowels, their origins, too," that spurs Jefferson to order a brisk wine and extra whisky rations for the canal men. Moeckel's touch is lyric and light, but the poem is full of psychological insight. Beneath the abundance of the natural world is "the strafe & groan" of all growth, "that hammer / no hand ever bears." To follow the invitation to origins would be dangerous for a man like Jefferson, and so he "turn[s] for home," where he can restore the "siltslappy" wildness of the natural world to his own sense of domestic order and largesse—a gesture that would, finally, not be without consequence.

Elizabeth Seydel Morgan (1939) is the author of five books of poetry, most recently *Spans: New and Selected Poems.* She received the Philabaum Poetry Award for *Without a Philosophy* and was a finalist for a Library of Virginia Literary Award for *On Long Mountain.* She has also received a Richmond Magazine Pollak Award and the Carole Weinstein Poetry Prize. In short fiction, she has awards from *Virginia Quarterly Review* and the *Southern Review.*

"Symmetry": In lean, elegantly fulfilled couplets, Elizabeth Seydel Morgan explores the binaries by which Jefferson attempted to sustain the "balancing act" that would allow him to live with the paradoxical and, perhaps even to him, disturbing aspects of his thought and actions. Like the pans of a scale, each pair of Morgan's lines pitches sometimes precarious extremes: left and right wings, head and heart (a reference to an infatuated letter Jefferson wrote to the married Maria Cosway), public and private, church and state, "the time for action and the time for thought." Jefferson disliked argument; as he wrote to fellow Virginian Charles Yancey in 1816, "I wish to avoid all collisions of opinion with all mankind." Yet he also knew its value, writing to P. H. Wendover just a year earlier that "difference of opinion leads to enquiry, and enquiry to truth." In its final couplet, "Symmetry" confronts the fact that, whatever Jefferson might have thought in any given moment about the paths that lead to "truth," his own balancing act (enslaved persons in the wings, Jefferson under the dome) involved, by necessity, obdurate dimensions defying neat categorization.

Carol Muske-Dukes (1945) is the author of fourteen books of poetry and prose, most recently the poetry collection *Twin Cities*. She is Professor of English and Creative Writing at the University of Southern California and former Poet Laureate of California. Her honors include a Guggenheim Fellowship, Pushcart Prizes, and appearances in *Best American Poetry*. She was a National Book Award poetry finalist in 2003 and is a poetry reviewer for the *Los Angeles Times*.

"Monticello": In *The Poetics of Space*, French phenomenologist Gaston Bachelard associates rationality with the roof of a house and irrationality with the cellar. "When we dream of the heights we are in the rational zone of intellectualized projects," he writes. "But for the cellar, the impassioned inhabitant digs and re-digs, making its very depth active." In Carol Muske-Dukes's poem, a visit to Monticello's dome room creates a compelling feeling of being inside Jefferson's idealized "brain," its octagonal shape allowing for few shadowy corners, its circular windows and imported skylight suffusing the room with as much light as possible, and the elevation permitting what might be thought of as a God's-eye view of the property below. Muske-Dukes doesn't forget the machinery of the rest of the house, however, reminding us of the "beautifully forged chains" of invention, tradition, custom, and law that perforce involved tyranny as well as freedom. The poem affords a glimpse into "a brain that invented America" in part by imagining (and living, on some levels) "its opposite." Muske-Dukes pays homage to Jefferson's imperfect vision, which was nonetheless capable of seeing "America, ongoing, invented" beyond the particulars of his moment and into "our / cyber-world, an inter-net of human nature, noble, vile." It is a world that technology makes, for individuals, both more democratized and more vulnerable, more connected but also, in some ways, less humanly accountable.

Amy Newman (1957) is the author of five books of poetry, most recently *On this Day in Poetry History.* She teaches at Northern Illinois University.

"To Avoid Thinking of Betsey Walker Reclining in a Bedroom at John Coles's Plantation, Thomas Jefferson Imagines the Orchard at Monticello,": Betsy Walker was the wife of Jefferson's school friend John ("Jack") Walker. In 1768, when Jefferson was twenty-five, John received an appointment in New York and asked his friend Thomas to look in on his wife while he was away. Whatever actually transpired between the two remained a more or less private matter until some sixteen years later, when Betsy reported to her husband Jefferson's earlier, repeated attempts to seduce her and word of the "Walker affair" made it into the press. Jefferson responded with a note to his lawyer and to Secretary of the Navy Robert Smith: "You will perceive that I plead guilty . . . that when young and single I offered love to a handsome lady. I acknolege [*sic*] its incorrectness." In Amy Newman's poem, we see the young Jefferson mapping his transgressive desires onto his orchards, though his ardor comes through powerfully in the sensual descriptions of petals, grapes, and "scandent vines," which blur with descriptions of Betsy's "fruitish blush." Clearly rational, moral thinking is overcome by the "secret and untamed" nature of desire, and while the "contradiction is not lost on him," it is interesting to contemplate the complexity of this earlier sexual encounter in light of Jefferson's later decisions about how to manage his erotic energy.

Lorine Niedecker (1903–1970), a second-generation modernist poet with strong ties to the objectivists, was born on Black Hawk Island in Wisconsin. Niedecker didn't publish her first collection until she was in her forties, and although she was much admired by her peers, she has in some respects been underappreciated, a circumstance ameliorated by the appearance of her *Collected Poems* in 2002. Although she only published four collections during her lifetime, she is now recognized for her wit, compression, and devotion to a singular poetic vision.

From "Thomas Jefferson": Excerpted here are sections from a longer poem, "Thomas Jefferson," comprising nineteen parts. A poet of place and politics, privacy and history, Niedecker often wrote about historical and literary figures from her reading, and although her style is terse, elliptical, and condensed, her subjects (Charles Darwin, Mary Shelly, John and Abigail Adams) are figures rife with contradictions. In an essay on Niedecker for the Academy of American Poets, Elizabeth Willis writes, "Niedecker herself was rich with complications—an ambitious poet who chose to live almost entirely outside professional networks; a localist fascinated with Lawrence of Arabia; a Marxist who owned property; a folk mannerist, setting the literary within the equally complex beauty of the commonplace." Shifting point of view, often sampling from Jefferson's work and her own reading, Niedecker's valedictory impression of the aging Jefferson allows lists, objects, and fragments from letters and other texts to speak volumes about the "die-down" of even the fullest life.

Debra Nystrom (1954) is the author of four books of poetry, including the forthcoming *Night Sky Frequencies.* She teaches in the Creative Writing Program at the University of Virginia. Her work has appeared in numerous anthologies and magazines, including the *American Poetry Review,* the *Kenyon Review,* the *New Yorker, Plough-shares, Slate,* and *Yale Review.* She has received honors and awards from *Best American Poetry, Five Points, Virginia Quarterly Review, Shenandoah,* the Virginia Commission for the Arts, and the Library of Virginia.

"Green-Winged Teals": In "Green-Winged Teals," Debra Nystrom's speaker is Meriwether Lewis, who led the Corps of Discovery, also later called the Lewis and Clark Expedition, into territory acquired by Jefferson in the Louisiana Purchase. In addition to attending to commercial interests (could the country be navigated by water to the Pacific, opening trade opportunities with Asia, for instance?), Jefferson charged Lewis with other tasks: mapping the terrain, sending back samples of indigenous flora and fauna, and forming trade relationships with and recording the languages of the Native American peoples encountered along the way. The expedition commenced in May 1804, and in 1805 the party found themselves camped among the hospitable Mandan Native Americans in North Dakota. Nystrom depicts Lewis in a private moment, observing a species of migrating bird and reporting on its habits by letter to the president. It is hard not to see the green-winged teal as a surrogate for Lewis himself, far from home and weighted with almost impossible responsibilities. Could he, Nystrom speculates, have longed, at some point, to be free of Jefferson's assignments of mapping and naming and trailblazing, burdens which may have contributed to his suicide (or possible murder) just four years later?

Simon Ortiz (1941), a member of the Acoma Pueblo tribal community, is Regents Professor at Arizona State University. Almost everything he writes, speaks, and publishes is from the point of view of his Indigenous heritage, of which he has said: "Without the USA's realization and acceptance of Indigenous America, there is only Euro-American invasion, occupation, conquest." His awards include two fellowships from the National Endowment for the Arts, a Lannan Foundation Artist in Residence Award, and the Golden Tibetan Antelope Prize for International Poetry.

"Freedom and the Lie: Monticello and Thomas Jefferson: Plan": Considered to be one of the greatest achievements of Jefferson's presidency, the Louisiana Purchase more than doubled the size of the nation. In a message to Congress in 1803, Jefferson said that the purchase made way for "our posterity, and a wide-spread field for the blessings of freedom and equal laws." Procuring that "freedom" and expansion, however, involved the appropriation of lands that had been inhabited, often for centuries, by native peoples. In paternal fashion, as he wrote in a letter to William H. Harrison, Jefferson hoped to "live in perpetual peace with the Indians, to cultivate an affectionate attachment from them." He went on to say, however, that if any tribe resisted his plan for incorporation or removal, "we presume that our strength and their weakness is now so visible that they must see we have only to shut our hand to crush them." Simon Ortiz's poem confronts the "lie" in the letter of any law professing freedom while ready at the same time to swiftly suppress or remove it. Ortiz, who was born into the Acoma Pueblo tribe and grew up speaking Keresan, offers a poem that resounds with the keening lament of oral tradition and of voices silenced by usurpation and exile.

Nathaniel Perry (1979) is the author of *Nine Acres*. He lives with his family in rural Southside Virginia, only about an hour and a half from Monticello, and is the editor of the *Hampden-Sydney Poetry Review*.

"Axis Mundi": In seven elegant Italian quatrains (envelope stanzas in iambic pentameter), Nathaniel Perry explores how gardening (in particular, the cultivation of a kind of spinach that Jefferson also grew at Monticello) necessitates continual surrender and reevaluation: "I try my best to sway // the wind and sun and rain, but really just switch / what they will fall on." The tidy stanzas whose lines sometimes straddle and overrun line breaks are themselves like plots of earth, tossed by wind or, perhaps, overgrown by weeds. By titling the poem "Axis Mundi," Perry conflates plant, house, and body, suggesting that all growth (of vegetables, ideas, buildings, nations) involves experimentation—risks and failures and victories in the attempt to discover a way to evolve, an "idea that works."

Kiki Petrosino (1979) is the author of two books of poems, *Fort Red Border* and *Hymn for the Black Terrific.* She is Associate Professor of English and Director of the Creative Writing Program at the University of Louisville. Her poems have appeared in *Best American Poetry,* the *Los Angeles Review of Books,* the *New York Times, Tin House, Fence,* and elsewhere. She is founder and coeditor of *Transom,* an online poetry magazine.

From "Mulattress": This poem is part five of a series from Kiki Petrosino's second collection, *Hymn for the Black Terrific.* The lines of each poem in the series end with, in sequence, the words of Jefferson's description of the Negro from Query XIV of *Notes on the State of Virginia:* "They secrete less by the kidnies, and more by the glands of the skin, which gives them a very strong and disagreeable odour." In the section presented here, the speaker addresses Jefferson; she talks about "your house," Monticello, and recounts some of what she has felt on a tour of the historical site. The voice is colloquial, intimate, and bristling with anger, irony, and dark humor. At every turn, Petrosino spins Jefferson's words to new, indicting uses: "You speak *less by* / the declarations of the body . . . / . . . *& more* / by your French partitioned doors." The poem closes with a paradox that is suffused with both wit and compassionate pity: "You're so sharp *& disagreeable* / to hold. *Je t'adore.*" By turning what is perhaps the most offensive part of an offensive sentence into an expression of love in the language of France, a country whose politics and culture so heavily influenced Jefferson's notions of America, Petrosino masterfully evokes in the reader a throng of responses that range from outrage to forgiveness.

Paisley Rekdal (1970) is the author of a book of essays, *The Night My Mother Met Bruce Lee;* a hybrid-genre photo-text memoir entitled *Intimate;* and four books of poetry: *A Crash of Rhinos, Six Girls without Pants, The Invention of the Kaleidoscope,* and *Animal Eye,* which was winner of the University of North Texas Rilke Prize. Her work has received a Guggenheim Fellowship, a National Endowment for the Arts Fellowship, two Pushcart Prizes, and two inclusions in the *Best American Poetry* series.

"Monticello Vase": With penetrating lucidity, Paisley Rekdal's poem gives an extraordinarily vivid virtual tour of "the Monticello I have never visited." As the speaker moves from public to private rooms, she visits spaces within spaces (portraits, maps, wine bottles), suggesting that there are ultimately unvisitable, invisible, or unknowable "corners" in Jefferson's house. By the time we arrive at "the smallest of these rooms," we locate the vase of the poem's title. The scene depicted on the vase (meant to commemorate the Lewis and Clark Expedition) is one of devastation and captivity—slaughtered buffalo, "great chains / or waves, bodies linked together by the leg, / a wolf between them snapping at a man / who grips him by the ears." These lines refer to a phrase Jefferson used at least twice to describe the difficulty of slavery as he saw it, as in a letter to John Holmes in 1820: "But, as it is, we have the wolf by the ear, and we can neither hold him, nor safely let him go." Jefferson likely took the phrase from Suetonius's biography of the Roman emperor Tiberius; here, Rekdal juxtaposes it with the story of Caractacus, a Saxon king whose eloquence saved him from Roman slavery. This palimpsest of classical, American, animal, and human allusions reminds the reader that whatever Jefferson was able to *say* about freedom always belied what he could or would not say, the truths beyond "reported speeches."

Mary Ann Samyn (1970), is the author of five collections of poetry, including, most recently, *My Life in Heaven,* winner of the 2012 *Field* Poetry Prize. She is Professor of English and Director of the MFA Program in Creative Writing at West Virginia University.

"Heirloom": Monticello is, of course, full of heirlooms, both Jefferson's own and those of other temporary and permanent denizens of the property. Some of these items descended to Jefferson's heirs when he died; others were sold off when the family lost the debt-ridden Monticello after Jefferson's death. Still other artifacts were lost and then restored to the family or replicated, even as objects of importance to the estate's enslaved people have been gradually excavated from Mulberry Row and environs. But as Mary Ann Samyn suggests, an heirloom does not need to be an object; human beings can be and were considered property. Likewise, an unrecorded talisman, a private moment or inkling, anything dropped or "set down, as on a tray, and carried away" can be as evocative an inheritance as a painting, piece of furniture, or scrap of embroidery. Samyn, stating that grief is "[i]tself an heirloom, held up, handed down," finally challenges any notion that time will "absolve" the lost and missing truths: "There is no cure but time, and for time, no cure." Her poem makes a guarded claim for poetry in attempting to bring us to the brink of the unspeakable, if not actually to speak it: "History begins to come true as we tell it. / This is the spot where."

Chet'la Sebree (1988) is the 2014–16 Stadler Fellow at Bucknell University's Stadler Center for Poetry. She is currently working on her first collection, which delves into identity, sexuality, and the life of Sally Hemings.

"Asylum from Grief, September 1795": Chet'la Sebree's sonnet, spoken in the voice of Sally Hemings, talks back to Jefferson's "A Dialogue between the Head and the Heart" letter, written to the married Maria Cosway when the newly widowed Jefferson became infatuated with her while living in Paris. In the well-known missive, Jefferson depicts a conversation between his head and his heart, his reason and his passion, in an attempt to resolve the tensions between what he felt to be moral, reasonable, and ethical, on one hand, and what would be true to the amorous desires of a still youthful man, on the other. Jefferson, as history has proven, stayed true to his vow not to remarry after his wife Martha's death, but he found a loophole by becoming sexually involved with his young slave, Sally Hemings. Sebree dates her poem in 1795, the year Hemings gave birth to her second child of six (four of whom lived to adulthood), all apparently fathered by Jefferson. Hemings was the half-sister of Martha Jefferson—whose father had several children with his slave Betty—and it was said that the two resembled one another. The closing couplet speaks to Jefferson's belief that blacks would benefit from admixture with whites. By off-rhyming "mourned" and "yours," Sebree suggests that while Jefferson may have found much needed asylum in his relationship with Hemings, the word "asylum" takes on a different meaning in relation to her situation.

Ravi Shankar (1975) is the author of seven books and chapbooks of poetry, including *What Else Could it Be: Ekphrastics and Collaborations*. He is the founding editor of *Drunken Boat,* a Professor of English at Central Connecticut State University and in City University of Hong Kong's international MFA program, and Chairman of the Connecticut Young Writers Trust. A Pushcart Prize winner, he has appeared on NPR, the BBC, and in the *New York Times, Caravan,* and the *Paris Review.*

"Thomas Jefferson in Kathmandu": For "Thomas Jefferson in Kathmandu," Ravi Shankar chooses terza rima, the intricate chain-rhymed tercet form that Dante Alighieri used in *The Divine Comedy.* Shankar's sojourner finds himself in Nepal, across the world from Monticello but thumbing Jefferson's "visage on a nickel" and musing on his own experience of "TJ" over time—from the years spent going through "the whole gamut of adolescent / failure and triumph" in a high school named for Jefferson to his later time as a student at Jefferson's University of Virginia. As the speaker moves among trekkers and seekers and stalls of Himalayan masks, he runs through a range of paradoxical scenarios and considers why, as an Indian-American who has suffered from prejudice in the United States, he feels more at home "in a country ruled by Maoists / and

Marxists than I do in the designer // shining city on the hill." He admits that despite all of his pondering, he can't "see clearly what has succeeded and what failed / in the grand American experiment," but as he gives his nickel to a beggar he realizes that if "honesty is the first chapter in the book of wisdom, / then its epilogue must be compassion. Not power."

Ron Slate (1950) has published two collections of poems: *The Incentive of the Maggot,* a National Book Critics Circle Award nominee, and *The Great Wave.* He recently became a board member of Mass Humanities, the Massachusetts state affiliate of the National Endowment for the Humanities.

"Cut-and-Paste Republic": As with most of the forces that shaped Jefferson's life, religion (including the question of whether God exists) was something about which he held myriad and sometimes contradictory opinions. But certainly his belief in the separation of church and state, documented in Query XVII of his *Notes on the State of Virginia* and in the Virginia Statute for Religious Freedom adopted in 1786, helped to shape the fledgling nation. In 1819/1820, Jefferson undertook to extract excerpts from the New Testament to create his own version of the Gospels, an effort he would call *The Life and Morals of Jesus of Nazareth.* Slate's take on Jefferson's project highlights the parallels between Jefferson's notions of Jesus—whose divinity he denied but whose moral teachings he revered—and his (perhaps uncertain) belief that a rational Republic could be pieced together out of disparate forces by removing whatever impeded such a conception. By the time Slate concludes his poem, we see Jefferson himself assuming with perhaps unconscious pride the role of creator, a man—as he wrote to Ezra Stiles Ely in 1819—"of a sect by myself, as far as I know."

Ron Smith (1949) is the author of *Running Again in Hollywood Cemetery, Moon Road,* and *Its Ghostly Workshop.* He is Writer-in-Residence and George Squires Chair of Distinguished Teaching at St. Christopher's School in Richmond, Virginia, as well as Adjunct

Associate Professor at the University of Richmond. He is the Poetry Editor for *Aethlon: The Journal of Sport Literature*. In 2014, he was named Poet Laureate of the Commonwealth of Virginia.

"Mr. Jefferson Speaks of Rapture": In 1767, Thomas Jefferson first saw Natural Bridge, a majestic gorge in Rockbridge County, Virginia. He subsequently bought it as part of a 157-acre tract of land. Moved by its beauty and recognizing it as a national treasure, Jefferson held on to the property even through hard times; it was sold after his death to help settle his significant debts. In "Mr. Jefferson Speaks of Rapture," Ron Smith describes Jefferson's initial visit to the bridge, an experience Jefferson recounted in his *Notes on the State of Virginia*. Although Jefferson can't help but respond to this astonishing natural creation with a rational list of measurements and calculations ("He always / provides a number of numbers"), Smith also shows us how much the reasonable, enlightened Jefferson was actually allied with the Romantics in his susceptibility to "the sublime." The moment, depicted in the *Notes* and in Smith's poem, when Jefferson falls to his knees and creeps to the edge to look over into the "abyss," only to be struck by a violent headache, recalls the stolen boat episode in Wordsworth's *Prelude*. Not without a strong thread of humor, Smith shows Jefferson recovering, recollecting from the relative tranquility of his writing desk the "intolerable" rapture of his own emotions.

R. T. Smith (1947) is the author of twenty collections of poems and stories, most recently *In the Night Orchard*. Writer-in-Residence at Washington and Lee University, Smith has received two Library of Virginia Literary Awards, the Carole Weinstein Award, and four Pushcart Prizes.

"Scuppernongs": A connoisseur of wine for most of his adult life, Jefferson naturally tried his hand at creating his own vineyard at Monticello after studying viticulture on his European travels. Although he struggled to establish European grapes in Virginia, he did have success growing and making wine from the scuppernong, which was perhaps introduced to him in 1817 by General John Cocke, who wrote in his diary of that year that he had "sent Mr. Jefferson some wine made from the Scuppernong grape of North Carolina." In his poem, R. T. Smith imagines Jefferson strolling through his vineyards at dusk and meditating on the virtues of this native muscadine—hardy, "dusky, Southern, its ruminant juices rife / with a sweetness indigenous to any / Edenic muscadine tribe." Although by the time he was growing the scuppernong grape at Monticello Jefferson was already aging and his wife had been dead for over thirty years, something about the "dusky" scuppernong (and his vain struggle "to mate / the Old World delicates to *vitus / vulpina*") has him remembering her with a certain indulgent melancholy, even as he turns toward home and "the thought of . . . his threadbare mourning shawl // already warmed by Sally's serving hands."

Tracy K. Smith (1972) is the author of three books of poetry: *The Body's Question,* winner of the Cave Canem Poetry Prize; *Duende,* winner of the James Laughlin Award of the Academy of American Poets and an Essence Literary Award; and, most recently, *Life on Mars,* winner of the 2012 Pulitzer Prize. Her memoir, *Ordinary Light,* was published in 2015.

"Monticello": The nocturnal, oneiric scene Smith creates in "Monticello" is at once piercingly personal and powerfully archetypal. While the poem could well be imagining a historical brother and sister, denizens of a Jefferson-era Monticello, whose father's own family tree is vexed by the intricacies of enslavement and manumission, the orchard Smith evokes also resembles Eden, with its sourceless Father ("Brother, / Do you ever wonder what created our father?") and its fruit-heavy tree, ponderous with strange consequence. The poem also feels strikingly contemporary, potentially depicting twenty-first century siblings in an exchange that interrogates the fear that might cause an "emancipated" person to "falter" in the face of cultural forces bent on hatred, racism, ignorance, and evil. By transposing the biological minting of a father's face onto the faces of a nation (one thinks, of course, of Jefferson's face on all those nickels), Smith has written a poem that speaks with subtle psychological insight into tensions that existed in eighteenth-century Albemarle County and are still disturbingly, abidingly present today.

Willard Spiegelman (1944) is the author of ten volumes of prose, most recently *Seven Pleasures: Essays on Ordinary Happiness* and *Senior Moments.* He was Editor-in-Chief of the *Southwest Review* from 1984–2015 and Hughes Professor of English at Southern Methodist University in Dallas. He has received grants from the Guggenheim, Rockefeller, Bogliasco, and Amy Clampitt Foundations and the National Endowment for the Humanities. He has been a frequent contributor to the *Wall Street Journal.*

"Prairie Rotunda": Thomas Jefferson's Pantheon-inspired Rotunda, its adjoining Lawn, pavilions, and gardens, and Jefferson's nearby Monticello together form one of only three manmade UNESCO World Heritage sites in the United States. Over the years, a number of other colleges and universities—among them Vanderbilt, Duke, MIT, and Tsinghua University in Beijing—have constructed their own Rotunda and Lawn–inspired structures and spaces. Willard Spiegelman's poem describes one such replica, Dallas Hall, offering "dominion / over sprawling fields of Johnson grass" at Southern Methodist University. In undulating stanzas that evoke Jefferson's famously elegant and durable serpentine walls, which mark off various walkways and gardens around the UVA Lawn, Spiegelman's poem recounts, with no small amount of humor, the provenance of SMU's "Texas-sized" homage to Jefferson's iconic building: "The Pantheon? More like University-as-Mall." When SMU's then-president looked out "at nothing, a shack and a / sad, deserted mule barn" in the early twentieth century and saw it as the future sight of Dallas Hall, his wife called him crazy. That he proved her wrong is a testament, Spiegelman points out, to a tenacious nexus of "[a]uthority, nature, / power, and reason" that "Mister Jefferson would have / understood."

Arthur Sze (1950) is the author of nine books of poetry, including most recently *Compass Rose.* He is Professor Emeritus at the Institute of American Indian Arts, where he taught for twenty-two years. His awards include the Jackson Poetry Prize, a Lannan Literary Award, and a Lila Wallace-Reader's Digest Writer's Award. He was the first Poet Laureate of Santa Fe (2006–8) and is currently a Chancellor of the Academy of American Poets.

"Sight Lines": The speaker in Arthur Sze's "Sight Lines" is walking a stretch of land outside of Sante Fe, New Mexico, where he can see the Río Nambe and "the snowpack in the Sangre de Cristos . . . already dwindled before spring"—observations he might have made at the time of the Louisiana Purchase. Other things he sees, however, reflect changes since that time: Los Alamos, for example, is now the site of a national laboratory where, among other things, scientists conduct work on the design of nuclear weapons. Sze makes the bold stroke of not attempting an unimpeded view of Monticello and Jefferson from where he stands, instead reversing the point of view: "no one could anticipate this distance from Monticello." Equally striking is the poem's extension beyond history, into a future-present only made possible by the reverie of imagination. Floating logos over topos, eros over polis, the speaker plays out the "sight" of his lines of poetry to "arrive at a space that no longer needs autumn or spring— / . . . / though you are visiting Paris, you are here at my fingertips."

Larissa Szporluk (1967) is the author of five books of poetry, most recently *Traffic with Macbeth.* She teaches creative writing at Bowling Green State University and was awarded a Guggenheim Fellowship in 2009.

"Pursuit": Surely aware of Jefferson's obsession with horticulture, Larissa Szporluk endows the vegetable world with a provocative mix of agency and captivity, coyness and helplessness. On one hand, her plants "run for the light"; on the other, they can "never leave bed." Even the grapes "are asleep," but in their seeming somnambulant state they are secretly "turning the truth into serum." By now the reader has enough information to connect these cultivated plants with other entities, including humans, who are stuck in "bed" at Monticello. Szporluk complicates her closet drama by personifying Happiness and bringing her onstage for a sip of truth serum, which Happiness pays for with her looks, her mobility, and finally her "right mind." The ending is provocative. On one hand, the poem has made clear that despite their pursuit of truth and light, the cultivars of Monticello can't escape their master's "pursuit of happiness," which for them means a kind of surrender to captivity. If Happiness (as object) drinks the Kool-Aid, she's unable to own property (including herself) and is unable to cross its boundaries. If we take Happiness as a kind of rogue double-agent, on the other hand, another reading becomes possible: it is "that man" who must realize that, though Happiness may not possess property, neither can she be "crossed," or obstructed, in her parallel pursuit of truth.

Tess Taylor (1977) is the author of a poetry chapbook, *The Misremembered World,* and a full-length collection, *The Forage House,* which was a finalist for the Believer Poetry Award. Taylor serves on the board of the National Book Critics Circle, reviews books for NPR's *All Things Considered,* and is Professor of English and Creative Writing at Whittier College.

"Graveyard, Monticello": "Graveyard, Monticello" comes from Tess Taylor's debut collection of poems, *The Forage House.* A white descendant of Thomas Jefferson, Taylor explores in this volume the fragments of her personal and contextual histories (part of her research was accomplished at Monticello at the International Center for Jefferson Studies), creating what Robert Pinsky has called an "epic" of courageous range. This poem opens in the graveyard on the grounds of Monticello, where Jefferson is buried along with ancestors of the author and others. Mixed in among descriptions of the place itself are "roving, grieving" musics from other places and times, particularly from parts of Appalachia, where some of Taylor's family lived and which comprised the "old west" to "these colonials." The quoted sentence, "My two hands grubbed," comes from notes in Jefferson's own hand regarding the work he considered necessary to prepare a burial plot for his friend and brother-in-law Dabney Carr. Carr's re-internment to the Monticello site from Shadwell was the start of the cemetery that formed around it, a site of exclusion as well as inclusion—like any poem, like any history or attempt at historical reclamation.

Brian Teare (1974) is the author of five books of poetry, most recently *The Empty Form Goes All the Way to Heaven*. After over a decade of teaching and writing in the San Francisco Bay Area, he is currently Assistant Professor at Temple University in Philadelphia, where he runs the micropress Albion Books. His book *Companion Grasses* was a finalist for the 2014 Kingsley Tufts Award.

"Double Sonnet for Monticello's Grounds": Inseparable from the mansion and other buildings at Monticello are its various gardens, decorative and edible, in which Jefferson took an avid and, when he could, hands-on interest—keeping for over fifty years a garden ledger book recounting everything from row spacing to bloom times to when particular vegetables should be brought to table. Brian Teare's double sonnet borrows language from Jefferson's instructions to various overseers and family members regarding, among other things, boxes of hawthorns that he had sent to Monticello (some 4,000 from a Georgetown nursery in 1805), with specifics about when to plant them and when to keep them in what he called "the nursery of thorns" until planting conditions were more favorable. Teare floats the language of Jefferson's letters and garden book over another "experiment," a private one having to do with Jefferson's own "grafted," mixed, and complicated family tree. Trellising his paired loose sonnets on the armature of a suspended syllogism ("If . . . if . . ."), Teare implicates the births and deaths of a myriad of offspring in and among notes about horticulture, suggesting that a kind of magical thinking as much as any rational logic lay behind these endeavors.

Natasha Trethewey (1966) served two terms as Poet Laureate of the United States, from 2012–14. Winner of the Pulitzer Prize for *Native Guard: Poems,* Trethewey is the author of four other poetry collections and has garnered many other prestigious awards, including the Poet Laureateship of Mississippi, a fellowship from the National Endowment for the Arts, and a Guggenheim Fellowship. She is the Robert W. Woodruff Professor of English and Creative Writing at Emory University.

"Enlightenment": The portrait of Jefferson that Natasha Trethewey refers to in "Enlightenment," an 1805 painting made by Gilbert Stuart, hangs in the Entrance Hall at Monticello and is considered to be not only one of Gilbert's finest works but a very convincing likeness of Jefferson. Trethewey, the daughter of a Caucasian father and an African American mother, uses the portrait's striking contrasts of light and shade to trigger an account of her speaker's gradual "enlightenment" about Jefferson's relationship with Sally Hemings, from her father's early rationalizations to her in childhood to her adult awareness not only of the truth of Jefferson's affair but also of the complicated reasons her father may have had for wanting to justify "our story." Even as father and daughter "take in how much has changed" (talk of Sally Hemings on a recent house tour, for instance), Trethewey shows us that Jefferson's legacy of racial inequity "links us—white father, black daughter— / even as it renders us other to each other."

David Wojahn (1946) is the author of eight books of poetry, most recently *World Tree,* which was awarded the Lenore Marshall Prize by the Academy of American Poets. He has been the recipient of numerous awards and honors, among them a Guggenheim Fellowship, the Poets' Prize, and two fellowships from the National Endowment for the Arts. He teaches at Virginia Commonwealth University and in the MFA in Writing Program of Vermont College of Fine Arts.

"Jefferson Composing His Bible": When approached about composing a poem for this anthology, David Wojahn responded immediately with an interest in exploring Jefferson's redaction of the New Testament to create what has become known as the Jefferson Bible. He explained that growing up in a Unitarian church, he'd heard much about Jefferson's Bible, from which Jefferson removed mention of the miraculous and supernatural, keeping only what he thought could be plausibly considered "fact." Wojahn's poem shows us Jefferson in the act of cutting out John 11, which depicts the raising of Lazarus from the dead. The poem itself is a collage of sorts, full of samplings—echoes of Lincoln, shout-outs to famous paintings of Lazarus, quotations from Jefferson's own descriptions of the project, and a final allusion to Robert Lowell's "Walking in the Blue," a poem about aging in a mental hospital ("We are all old-timers, / each of us holds a locked razor"). As Wojahn asks us to consider the Jefferson Bible, his rationale for it, and the cut-up Bibles that he used to create it, a kind of methodical violence in his handiwork comes through, as does a sense of how *modern* the process was. As Wojahn wrote to me, it was "collage-making, pure and simple, artistry of a sort" that compellingly evokes the processes by which conceptions of America are always being redacted, revised, and created anew.

Charles Wright (1935) is the author of over twenty books of poetry and prose, most recently *Caribou: Poems.* He is Professor Emeritus at the University of Virginia, where he taught for over two decades. His many awards include the Pulitzer Prize, the National Book Award, and the Bollingen Prize for Poetry. He was named United States Poet Laureate in 2014.

"Christmas East of the Blue Ridge": Charles Wright has called himself a "God-fearing agnostic," and "Christmas East of the Blue Ridge" is suffused with an uneasy yearning for divine visitation, as well as with Wright's other favored subjects: valediction; the turn of the seasons; the "vocabulary" of landscape and the zodiac; the "gall and first birth" not only of Christmas, the winter solstice, and the old year, but of the heart. Jefferson's Monticello makes what at first might seem a cameo appearance in the poem, but in the precise economy of Wright's work there are no random images. The region he's speaking of ("East of the Blue Ridge") is the site of the original colonies, and the half-moon hung over Jefferson's home "[h]ums like a Hottentot." The Hottentots were the Khoikhoi peoples of southwest Africa, a population known for their special worship of the moon and for their "clicking" language (thus the onomatopoeic term *Hottentot*, now considered derogatory), a tribe damaged and eventually destroyed by European invaders. Wright is surely conscious that Monticello functions metonymically in the context of his poem, a representation of our collective dishevelment and "[t]he alphabet of our discontent / [that] Keeps on with its letter, / gold on the black walls of our hearts . . ."

Kevin Young (1970) is the author of nine books of poetry and prose, most recently *Book of Hours,* a finalist for the Kingsley Tufts Poetry Award. The coeditor with Michael S. Glaser of *The Collected Poems of Lucille Clifton,* he is also Charles Howard Candler Professor of Creative Writing and English and Curator of Literary Collections and the Raymond Danowski Poetry Library at Emory University. He is currently the Holmes Visiting Poet at Princeton University.

"On Imagination": Named for the ship that brought her from Africa (the *Phillis*) by the family who bought her (the Wheatleys of Boston), Phillis Wheatley was born about a decade after Thomas Jefferson, although he long outlived her. Wheatley's talent and intelligence were recognized early on by her master and his family, and she was given a serious education including the Greek and Latin classics as well as English poets such as Alexander Pope and John Milton. The first African American woman to publish a book of poems, Wheatley was greatly admired by many in the United States and Europe, but Jefferson was not among that number; anxious as he was to prove that the young nation could "produce her full quota of genius," as he wrote in Query XIV of *Notes on the State of Virginia,* he considered Wheatley's poems "below the dignity of criticism." Kevin Young restores to readers the emerging poet as she negotiates her contradictory world as slave and "family member," African and enslaved person. Trapped as she is by her own circumstances, Wheatley is buoyed by "Faith // which lets me know what I must do" and by gratitude "for the Ink / . . . which I could flood the world with." Even if she cannot fly, her words can, and do. "I wait," she says, in Young's poem, itself a palpable embodiment of the poetic legacy she began.

Unless otherwise credited, all poems are copyright of their respective
authors. Grateful acknowledgment is made for permission to reprint
the following previously published works. Every attempt has been
made to contact copyright holders. The editor and publisher would
be interested in hearing from anyone not here acknowledged.

Lucille Clifton: "monticello" from *The Collected Poems of Lucille
Clifton.* © 1987 by Lucille Clifton. Reprinted by permission of the
Permissions Company, Inc., on behalf of BOA Editions Ltd, www
.boaeditions.org.
Kate Daniels: "Reading a Biography of Thomas Jefferson in the
Months of My Son's Recovery" first appeared in *poemmemoirstory.*
Rita Dove: "What Doesn't Happen" from *Sonata Mulattica.* W. W.
Norton & Company, New York, NY © 2009 by Rita Dove.
Reprinted by permission of the author.
Nick Flynn: "When I Was a Girl" first appeared in the *Kenyon Review.*
Robert Hass: "Monticello" [24 1.] from *Praise* by Robert Hass.
© 1979 by Robert Hass. Reprinted by permission of HarperCol-
lins Publishers.
Jennifer Key: "Jefferson's Daughters" from *The Old Dominion:
Poems* by Jennifer Key. © 2013 by the University of Tampa Press.
Reprinted by permission of the University of Tampa Press.
Lorine Niedecker: Excerpts from "Thomas Jefferson" from *Lorine
Niedecker: Collected Works,* edited by Jenny Penberthy. © 2002 by
the Regents of the University of California. Reprinted by permis-
sion of the University of California Press.
Kiki Petrosino: "Mulattress [5]" from *Hymn for the Black Terrific.*
© 2013 by Kiki Petrosino. Reprinted by permission of the Permis-
sions Company, Inc., on behalf of Sarabande Books, www.sara
bandebooks.org.
Ravi Shankar: "Thomas Jefferson in Kathmandu" first appeared in
Caravan.